OVERCOMING OCD'S GRIP

STRATEGIES TO CONQUER INTRUSIVE THOUGHTS
AND COMPULSIVE BEHAVIORS—REGAINING
CONTROL AND ENDING INTERFERENCE WITH
DAILY LIFE

JESSE HARPER

TABLE OF CONTENTS

Introduction   5

1. MEETING THE DISORDER: WHAT IS OCD?   9
Defining Obsessive-Compulsive Disorder   9
The Prevalence of OCD   12
The Impacts of OCD   15

2. THE BIG "WHY"?   19
The Science of OCD   19
Types of OCD   23
Misconceptions about OCD   25

3. MAGNIFYING THE SIGNS   29
OCD Symptoms: A Deep Dive   29
What Are Compulsions?   32
Identifying Intrusive Thoughts   34
Recognizing Your Triggers   35

4. INTO THE DOCTOR'S OFFICE   39
Diagnostic Criteria   40
The Diagnostic Process   42
Who Can Diagnose?   44
Seeking Professional Help   46

5. WHAT ARE MY OPTIONS?   49
Cognitive-Behavioral Therapy   50
Medication Management   53
Alternative and Complementary Therapies   55

6. EXPOSURE AND RESPONSE PREVENTION   60
What Are Exposure Therapy and ERP?   61
How Successful Is It?   63
Implementing ERP Techniques   66

7. MINDFULNESS AND SELF-COMPASSION   70
What Is Mindfulness?   71
The Definition of Self-Compassion   72

Reducing Anxiety through Present Moment
Awareness   75
Cultivating Self-Acceptance with OCD   77

8. OCD MANAGEMENT LIKE A PRO   79
   Common Coping Techniques   79
   Manage Triggers   82
   Dealing with Compulsions and Intrusive Thoughts   83
   Creating a Supportive Daily Routine   86
   Creating OCD-Friendly Routines   87

9. REBUILDING RELATIONSHIPS   89
   How OCD Impacts Relationships   90
   Improving Communication   92
   Fostering Empathy   94
   Asking for Support   97

10. EDUCATION AND ADVOCACY   99
    The Value of Advocacy   100
    Advocating for Yourself and Others   103
    Spreading OCD Awareness   106

11. RELAPSE PREVENTION   109
    What an OCD Relapse Looks Like   109
    Developing a Relapse Prevention Plan   112
    Inspiring Success Stories   115

12. FORWARD MOTION   119
    Setting and Achieving Personal Goals   120
    Reflecting on the Journey   123
    Embracing Life beyond OCD   126

    Conclusion   129
    References   133

INTRODUCTION

You know that moment when you're lying in your bed, just before sleep, when the shadows seem to start their dance across your ceiling and the anxieties quickly turn into monsters? For most, these pangs are fleeting. Even if they arise, they are quickly wiped away by a peaceful sleep. But for you, it becomes a full-stage production of your "what ifs" and "what could have been." You lie there in the dark, with this melody of intrusive thoughts wrecking your peace. And they also completely hijack your days. You know obsessive-compulsive disorder (OCD) and its suffocating grip of rigid rituals all too well. It's the endless loop of checking and double-checking, followed by the whispers of doubt that make you check again. That feeling can make the simplest tasks feel like walking across glass.

You've probably heard some people say that living with OCD is like walking uphill, but you know that it's more like clinging to the one grip on the smoothest, steepest face of a mountain. You feel like you're one misstep from a devastating collapse. You're carrying all this exhaustion, frustration, and soul-crushing weight of a reality that is a product of your thoughts. All you want is some semblance of normalcy, where order doesn't dictate your every waking moment and where routines are not in place to act as shackles.

I know that you've been clinging on to that rock face, but there is hope for you. You don't have to live like this forever. It's not a rescue chopper; it's you pulling yourself out of this. You can climb back, inch by inch, until you get out of this constant fight-or-flight mode and feel that tranquility wash over you once again. This book is your rope, a sherpa, and your map to getting your life back from the clutches of OCD.

Think of this book as a C.L.E.A.R path to your freedom.

- **Comprehension:** We will break down this ferocious beast that is OCD, which means looking at every part of its anatomy, understanding its triggers, and exposing its weaknesses. After this, there will be no more confusion or fear of the unknown. You will have a much clearer understanding of your own mind.
- **Looking at you:** We can't approach this as a one-size-fits-all journey. We will explore just how diverse OCD's landscape is, from the compulsive hand-washer to the mind trapped in a tangled mess of intrusive thoughts. This is where you will discover where you fit, your unique challenges, and comfort in knowing that you're not alone.
- **Empowerment:** This isn't about understanding; it's about gaining control. You will be equipped with strategies, from cognitive reframing to exposure therapy. These will be there for you to try and tame the awful thoughts and break free of compulsion.

- **Accessing growth:** It's not simply a matter of coping. This book is here to help you thrive. We will try and tap into the hidden strengths that you've honed while facing OCD, and we will turn that resilience into the fuel that will launch you into a place of personal growth. You will get to rediscover the joy, passion, and vibrancy that you have for life—the very thing OCD has kept hidden.
- **Recovery for life:** We will do our best to make sure that you don't experience relapse. Together, we will build a fortress of self-awareness and habits that will help you if this monster decides to wake up. By learning to navigate your OCD triggers with confidence in yourself, you will make great steps to leaving OCD in the past instead of letting it be a shadow looming over your future self.

This book isn't written by a distant expert, but it's from someone who has witnessed this climb from a very close perspective, someone who has felt the cold sweats at night and the doubt with every step. I didn't get a map, either, and I've had to make a lot of these steps feeling alone. I learned from my triumphs and my setbacks. So this won't just be a book from me to you; it will be the outstretched hand reaching for you, chanting at the same time that you *can* do this.

With that being said, if you make it through this book and still feel like you are clinging to that steep slope, you should contact a professional. It doesn't mean you are weaker than someone else; it just means that you need a few more climbing tools for your particular mountain. And if it ever feels like too much, no matter the stage of the journey, the strongest thing you can do is reach out.

The climb back from this is tough, but if you have the right tools and trust in yourself, you can reach the summit and enjoy the panorama of the life that you reclaimed. So when you're ready, take that first step. Remember, OCD doesn't define you. It empowers you. So turn the page and let's start that climb together.

MEETING THE DISORDER: WHAT IS OCD?

"It's like having mental hiccups. Mostly, we can function despite the "hiccups,"' but we're exhausted attempting to carry on as if they didn't exist."

— SHEILA CAVANAUGH

To truly get a grasp on the things you can do to manage OCD, you must understand the very nature of this disorder. Even if you have gotten a professional diagnosis, it's still likely that you're not fully educated on the ins and outs of OCD. So before we begin tackling the monster, we need to understand it. We have a lot of ground to cover, too, so let's dive in.

DEFINING OBSESSIVE-COMPULSIVE DISORDER

Think of all of this as a record player being stuck on the most unsettling song, playing repeatedly. Intrusive thoughts, anxieties, or mental images play over and over, which cause deep distress in all who experience them. This is the essence of the experience that we know as obsessive-compulsive disorder.

What is OCD?

The misconception is that OCD simply means that someone is a neat freak or they have a few interesting quirks. However, this is a very real mental health condition that comprises two key components: obsessions and compulsions.

Obsessions are the persistent, unwanted thoughts, fears, and images that you cannot seem to get under control. These intrusions can be about anything—from contamination by germs, to harming oneself or loved ones, to having things in perfect order. These thoughts will trigger feelings of anxiety and distress, and they never simply "go away."

Compulsions are the attempts that the afflicted person makes to quell the anxiety that is sparked by the obsession. These are the repetitive behaviors or mental acts that we feel driven to do because we feel like it manages the distress. Some will wash their hands obsessively while others need to ensure that things are in a perfect symmetrical order. My personal experience was with checking my locks repeatedly when leaving the house. These are the most common compulsions, and while they do bring temporary comfort, they eventually become time-consuming and interfere with daily life.

Signs and Symptoms of OCD: An Overview

At this point, we are likely aware that OCD is a massive web that brings together intrusive thoughts, anxieties, and repetitive behaviors. While the threads that comprise the web are different from person to person, there are some common symptoms that make us realize that we are not alone. So let's dive in briefly to what these symptoms and signs are.

- **Intrusive thoughts:** We have glanced over these already. They are the unwanted, persistent thoughts, worries, or images that bring distress and trigger the compulsions. These can range from fears and doubts to violent impulses or even distressing scenarios.
- **Anxiety and distress:** The intrusive thoughts will trigger significant feelings of anxiety and distress, which can make people feel extremely overwhelmed and uncomfortable.
- **Compulsions:** This is what we turn to in an attempt to manage the anxiety. Many will feel like they are anxious or in distress, but they will overlook that they are using repetitive behaviors or mental acts in an attempt to get relief from those obsessions.
- **Physical symptoms:** OCD can put so much mental strain on a person that it can show up in physical symptoms. Those afflicted can potentially feel things like fatigue, headaches, and muscle tension. It's like you've been working out while exhausted for days on end.
- **Emotional symptoms:** OCD can also wreak havoc on emotions. You might have feelings like guilt, shame, and isolation. On top of the cycle of intrusive thoughts and anxieties, you are also dealing with these negative emotions—and the worst part is being unable to share these struggles.

Does OCD Always Look the Same?

Let's take two people struggling with OCD. We have one that is focused on cleaning their hands every few minutes because they are terrified of germs. Meanwhile, the other person is constantly checking and rechecking their stove because they are afraid they left it on and are going to start a fire. While both are dealing with obsessions and compulsions, they look nothing alike to us.

While many think that OCD is a one-size-fits-all condition, you have to remember that just like our fingerprints, all our minds are unique. This means that the distress you feel and the outward expressions you show are going to fall on a very diverse spectrum of presentations.

So, because it's all vastly different, let's look at some of the common displays of OCD.

- **Contamination fears:** This is an overwhelming preoccupation with germs and cleanliness, leading to excessive cleaning.
- **Checking compulsions:** This is where one will check things repeatedly, like locks, appliances, or other things.
- **Symmetry and order obsessions:** Things have to be in order, balanced, or arranged in a very specific way.
- **Intrusive thoughts:** These are unwanted and upsetting thoughts that can include violence and harm.
- **Hoarding:** This happens when someone has a hard time getting rid of possessions because of an emotional attachment or a fear of future needs.

There are also several more that encompass mental rituals and counting compulsions to relationships to even obsession over one's morality. We will get into this more in this book but don't forget that OCD can wear many different hats.

THE PREVALENCE OF OCD

Now, we need to look at some of the metrics. Again, this will give you a better understanding of just how many people are struggling with this. We will also cover misdiagnoses and comorbidity.

How Many People Have OCD?

OCD is something that is veiled by misconceptions, and one of the biggest is how common it is. While most think that the condition is rare, it is much more nuanced. While more studies and research need to be done, we are still looking at around two to three million adults who are afflicted (Zauderer 2023).

However, while we think this is an issue that afflicts adults, OCD usually develops during childhood or adolescence. Because of this early manifestation, there is a discrepancy between those who are diagnosed and those who aren't. This leads to many people struggling for years with undiagnosed OCD because it's seen as a quirk during childhood. Furthermore, the stigma that surrounds mental health causes many to avoid getting help, especially during formative years. This only adds to the challenge of knowing just how many are out there living with OCD.

While the stats are important, they are just a glimpse into a truly complex issue. They also don't do enough to cover those who are afflicted without a diagnosis. The real importance is knowing that you are not alone in your climb. I have been there, and there are others out there, too. By shedding light on these numbers, we find a clearer path to understanding and supporting everyone with OCD.

OCD and Misdiagnosis

Trying to find the right treatment for OCD is like entering a labyrinth, and it's filled with misdiagnosis. So many people will end up with the wrong diagnosis, but what causes this?

First, OCD is a monster that wears many masks. As you can see, the signs and symptoms, you can see overlap with conditions like anxiety, depression, and even personality disorders. Therefore, a person with intrusive thoughts might mistakenly be diagnosed with generalized anxiety. Then a person who has obsessions about harming others might be misdiagnosed with a personality disorder.

Then we have to look at the other thing we have learned—that OCD doesn't always follow the stereotypical symptoms. Not everyone is washing hands or checking locks; they could be dealing with intrusive thoughts and mental rituals. This, too, can lead to misdiagnosis.

The good news is that we aren't doomed if there is a misdiagnosis. In actuality, we are a step in the right direction. Instead of finding fault in a misdiagnosis, we can look at this as a sign that what we are dealing with is being taken seriously and that it can be explored further. What also matters is that the earlier we work toward finding the right diagnosis, the sooner we can get effective treatment.

OCD and Comorbidity

By now, we have a lot of the basics of OCD locked down. However, sometimes, OCD isn't alone. It's often seen mingling with other conditions, which creates an even bigger web of struggle, known as comorbidity.

The simplest way to think about comorbidity is to think of Venn diagrams. Each circle is a condition, and the overlapping area is where they all come together in the afflicted person. And when it comes to OCD, several disorders occupy the overlapping space. So, let's get a better look at some of the other things that will overlap with OCD.

- **Anxiety disorders:** These frequently accompany OCD, with the most common being generalized anxiety and social anxiety. The constant worry and fear that comes from anxiety can add more fuel to the intrusive thoughts and compulsions of OCD.
- **Depression:** The darkness of depression can also be found in those with OCD. These will be through feelings like hopelessness and worthlessness. The symptoms of OCD often ramp up these feelings, making them far harder to manage.
- **Eating disorders:** Things like anorexia nervosa or bulimia are about rigid control and distorted body image issues, and these can overlap with OCD when it relates to food, weight, and appearance.
- **Attention deficit hyperactivity disorder (ADHD):** ADHD can cause issues with focus and impulse control, and they, too, can complicate how one manages their OCD. This happens because it can make it harder to stick to a therapy plan and avoid compulsions.
- **Personality disorders:** Certain personality disorders, like obsessive-compulsive personality disorder (OCPD), will have or mimic a lot of the same symptoms that OCD does, which can add a new challenge in diagnosis and treatment.

THE IMPACTS OF OCD

To close off our introduction to this disorder, we will explore how OCD affects us in different parts of our lives. From what should be mundane routines of our daily existence to the delicate areas of life, like relationships and even the pressure that it puts on our professional lives, the number of intrusive thoughts and compulsions can create a huge number of challenges.

On Daily Life

For a majority of those with OCD, our everyday activities pave the way for a minefield of triggers. Something as simple as making dinner can be hijacked by an endless routine of handwashing. Leaving the house becomes a drawn-out routine of checking to make sure everything is off or that the doors are locked. Even going to bed can be a nightmare if you're obsessed with cleanliness.

Everything is hijacked by endless fear, and the compulsions that we use to cope with the obsessions can consume hours of our day, robbing us of any moments of spontaneity and happiness.

The barrage of intrusive thoughts is constant, and it makes it almost impossible to concentrate, relax, or just enjoy the most basic of things. We lose our time management abilities, and even-tually, because we are so afraid of setting off those compulsions, we simply avoid things like our daily routines and social inter-actions.

On Relationships

Our relationships often take the biggest brunt of the impact of OCD. Romantic partners, friends, and even family can find them-selves caught up in this compulsive web we weave. They will give reassurance, join in on your compulsions, or they will just walk on eggshells around you to avoid potential triggers.

Because the dynamics are skewed, it can lead to a lot of resentment and misunderstandings. This will cause distance in relationships or difficulty in finding emotional connections. As a person who suffers from OCD, you might feel guilt because you feel like you're being a burden. And those around you will feel frustrated and helpless.

Communication breaks down because of anxieties and compulsion, which leads to isolation and lack of support.

On Professional Life

The professional world presents a different set of challenges for those with OCD. We are faced with the demands of deadlines, collaboration, and plenty of public interactions. Those things can elevate our anxieties and trigger more intrusive thoughts.

We are supposed to be focused on our work, but instead, that flow is disrupted by compulsions. More compulsions lead to decreased productivity and missed opportunities. In the professional setting, it can be easy to be afraid of judgment. There has been such a stigma on mental health until recently, which means there are still plenty of people who won't disclose their condition because they're afraid of being judged.

However, when no one knows about the condition, it makes it extremely difficult to navigate the challenges of the workplace or have people understand you. The added pressure to just be normal will lead to exhaustion and eventual burnout, which hinders the chances to grow professionally or achieve new career opportunities.

———

Remember, everything we have discussed in this chapter is just glimpses into the very complex world of OCD. Just like OCD is different for every person, it can impact different areas of our lives. It's important to approach your experience with compassion, along with the understanding that while there are others with OCD, they will feel things very differently than you. You also have to remember that there is a long road to recovery, especially as we begin to get to the causes of it.

With that being said, the overwhelming doubts, the endless cycle of compulsion, and the negative shadow that OCD casts leave you with a lot of questions that need answers.

Why does OCD have this grip on your life? What parts of your brain bring about this nightmare? How does the outside world play into those obsessions? What amplifies the fear, and what calms the storm? That's where we will turn our attention in the next chapter.

We will dive into the intricate workings of our brain, and we will explore how your unique background and your current environment shape how you deal with this struggle. Prepare yourself, as we are about to peel back the curtain on OCD and take the next step to reclaim your life.

THE BIG "WHY"?

"For me, it's an ever-present nagging feeling that something is just "not right." I can never really, truly 'make it right.' I have to learn to live with the all-consuming feeling of mental discomfort."

— LAURA MCCARTHY

Now that we've had a basic introduction, it's time to introduce you to the questions that you have in your head about OCD. These are the most common "why" questions from those dealing with this disorder. Our goal, by the end of this chapter, is for you to understand why OCD exists, what makes it so common, and the different types of OCD. This will give us a solid base that will help us proceed to the next part of this book.

THE SCIENCE OF OCD

To start our journey, we must look at the most important question: Where does OCD come from?

OCD, like many other mental health issues, can come from many places, and knowing what those places are can help you find what contributed to your struggles.

Psychological and Neurochemical Precedence

Like other mental health disorders, researchers and scientists have been hard at work to piece together the intricate puzzle that is OCD. While they are still trying to unveil the issue fully, they have been able to find some key factors that influence OCD's development. Let's look at a few of those things.

- **Brain connections misfiring:** Our brain is a network of roads. With OCD, some connections between the thinking and impulse control areas and the areas in habit and reward are under construction. It causes a miscommunication, which leads to obsessions and compulsions.
- **Chemical balancing act:** Our neurotransmitters (the chemical messengers in our brain) are crucial to our emotions and behaviors. Serotonin, which is involved with our mood and impulse control, is typically lower in people with OCD. Keep in mind that while this isn't a guaranteed cause, the imbalance can play a role in our obsessions and compulsions as we try to compensate for the lack of serotonin.
- **A problem with learning:** Our experiences can shape how we respond to our anxieties. This is often seen in situations like trauma or overly strict parenting. Because of these experiences, individuals will develop poor coping mechanisms, like compulsions.
- **Individual vulnerability:** We will dive into these in more detail in the next sections, but genetics and environmental

triggers also have their part in all this. Simply put, some people are going to be more prone to developing OCD thanks to those factors.

Genetic Factors

As stated when we wrapped the last section, genetics can also play a part in how you develop OCD. As we learn more about OCD, the more we see that there is a hereditary aspect where some genes are varied, which increases our chances of developing the disorder. Again, it's not guaranteed, but it can contribute to this.

We've started to see more evidence that those who have a close relative with OCD are significantly more at risk of developing it too. In the case of identical twins, who share their genes, we see that both of them have a higher chance of developing OCD. When it comes to fraternal twins, though, only one is susceptible. This leads us to look more at genetic influences, but the environment will still play a role.

We are also seeing more evidence that there may be specific genes that contribute to OCD, going back to the serotonin genes. So, there isn't just one gene that determines if someone will get it; there is a complex web of genetic variations.

Again, disposition isn't a guarantee. Also, understanding the genetic components of OCD doesn't set us up for a solution, but it's such an important piece of the puzzle. Having these pieces helps find better treatment options, which even eventually pave the way for developing preventative strategies.

Environmental Factors

While we may be predisposed to having OCD, our environment plays a major role in our growth. Our positive and negative life experiences can influence the likelihood of developing OCD, so let's look at some of those in more detail.

- **Stressful situations:** We all experience major life changes. Things like job loss or major shifts in our family and relationships can act as strong OCD triggers for those who are predisposed to it. The constant mental pressure we feel can fuel our existing anxieties, which leads to the reliance on compulsions to cope.
- **Traumatic experiences:** Traumatic events can leave deep scars on our psyche, and they can affect how our brains operate, making people more vulnerable to anxiety disorders, including OCD. With OCD and trauma, the individual is using rigid control and order to try and reclaim the sense of safety that was lost in the event.
- **Upbringing and family dynamics:** Traumatic events in childhood can cause OCD, but often overlooked are factors like overly strict parenting and harsh punishments for not meeting expectations. This fuels the fear of making mistakes, so the individual strives to make everything perfect. This can put the person at risk of developing OCD as a way to avoid disapproval.
- **The harsh world:** The world out there is rough. Things like social isolation and bullying are other factors that can set off OCD symptoms. Feeling like an outsider or having every step judged harshly can heighten anxiety. Because of this, the individual might lean into compulsions in an attempt to get reassurance.

And just like genetic factors, environmental factors don't automatically mean that the person will develop OCD. But the more we know, and the more threads of your OCD that you can find, the more effective you will be at finding support and treatment strategies.

TYPES OF OCD

Let's go back to something that we've said earlier. We have seen how OCD is displayed in the media. Usually, a person has a huge list of these compulsions. However, OCD is far more diverse and far less exuberant. So with this umbrella term that is obsessive-compulsive disorder, distinct types of OCD can live under it. Each type is characterized by its obsessions and compulsions. For this, we will dive into the three most common types and show their uniqueness and the common threads that unite them.

Pure O

While there are outwardly visible types, Pure O is not one of them. This operates solely in the person's mind. If you have Pure O, then you're filled with intrusive thoughts that cloud out almost all other thoughts. These thoughts can vary from violence and blasphemous thoughts to disturbing imagery. This is anything that revolves around questions of morality or existential questioning.

The difference with Pure O is that there are no visible compulsions. Instead, these rituals happen from a strictly mental standpoint. You might seek reassurance excessively, ruminate, or spend your time trying to disprove what you're thinking with logic. It's a constant mental battle that can debilitate you, and it often leaves you feeling isolated and like no one understands you.

Contamination OCD

If you are someone struggling with contamination OCD, the world is teeming with invisible threats. Your thoughts are in overdrive as you think about germs, dirt, and even bodily fluids, and you often magnify them to massive proportions. Because of this, you're triggered to clean relentlessly, and you've even begun to avoid leaving your sanitized space as much as possible.

Your compulsions are very noticeable. You might excessively wash your hands, shower multiple times a day, clean your home daily (or more), or constantly check for contaminants. It's this fear that leads to isolation, and it can even get in the way of a necessary activity, like eating.

ROCD

Our relationships mean so much, but Relationship OCD (ROCD) will bring a level of doubt and uncertainty that is hard to overcome. ROCD can have you questioning the very core of a relationship with intrusive thoughts.

You might find yourself constantly questioning your compatibility with your partner, the sexual attraction in the relationship, or even looking ahead to potential future happiness. These obsessions will lead to compulsions like seeking reassurance constantly, comparing your relationship to other relationships, or even testing your feelings. This compulsion puts a huge strain on yourself and your partner because they won't know how to navigate these thoughts with you. They might also feel attacked or that you don't trust them, which can hurt the relationship.

While these common types give you a general idea of how OCD is presented, you have to remember that this is a very intricate web with a myriad of individual threads. With OCD, it's very common to see the types blur together, and co-occurrences frequently happen. The common thread of them all, though, is that distressing, intrusive thoughts are always present, and the only way we can deal with them is through a compulsion.

MISCONCEPTIONS ABOUT OCD

As we've discussed, there are misconceptions about OCD. To help you get a better understanding of this affliction, we need to look at the myths and put them in their rightful place. So, let's start with the most common misconceptions about OCD.

1. **"OCD is only about being neat and organized."** While there are some whose compulsions will have them being overly clean and organized, that doesn't make the myth true. You've learned that obsessions live in a vast spectrum and that compulsions are how we try to deal with those obsessions. Therefore, it's not just about making sure things are neat.
2. **"Everyone is a little OCD."** The problem with mental health today is that it gets casually used to describe quirks or preferences. Anyone who says this has not experienced debilitating anxiety and the compulsions that will eat up most of their day. It's a disorder, not a personality trait to flaunt online.
3. **"OCD is caused by a bad upbringing or just being weak."** We spent the first half of this chapter talking about how this is a mental health condition that comes from a complex interplay of genetic, neurobiological, and environmental factors. So blaming someone's resolve or

their upbringing promotes stigma and causes a person to not seek help.

4. **"OCD makes a person violent or dangerous."** Think again to those with Pure O, and that's where you'll find your answer. The intrusive thoughts are there, but they rarely manifest themselves into harmful actions. Those with OCD are more likely to become victims rather than the dangerous ones.

5. **"People who have OCD just need to relax and get a hold of their thoughts."** If it was that easy, I'm sure none of us would be here right now. However, this isn't a matter of willpower. Intrusive thoughts are uncontrollable, and when you do try to control them, they often manifest into something more. This is a disorder that needs intervention and therapy over sheer willpower.

6. **"OCD is untreatable, and the afflicted are doomed for the rest of their lives."** There have been significant strides made in the field that allow those with OCD to manage their symptoms and take back some control of their lives. We can't make it go away, but we aren't doomed, either.

7. **"People with OCD are just faking it for attention."** This takes us back to the second myth. For those who are using it to describe a quirk they have, it is for attention. However, those dealing with OCD are not motivated by validation or attention. They would give anything to not be associated with it.

8. **"Talking about it makes it worse."** Open communication and support are so crucial for those dealing with OCD. Sharing feelings and experiences can help lead to better understanding, reduce stigma, and lead the way toward help.

By debunking the most common misconceptions, we can open up a more supportive and empathetic environment for ourselves. But now, what can we do to challenge the stigma of OCD?

Challenging the Stigma

Now that we know what it is, where it can come from, and the myths behind it, we have taken a great step in the right direction. So how can we make a difference and actively challenge the stigma around OCD?

- **Reframe the perspective:** Stop seeing your OCD as a burden and acknowledge that this is a part of who you are. While it has shaped who you are now, it's only a part of your internal landscape. That doesn't mean it's the thing that defines you.
- **Become your advocate:** Get as much knowledge as you can about OCD. Go beyond this book and learn more about the diverse presentations and treatment options. Then, don't be afraid to share this with loved ones and others you know. This will allow them to start challenging the stigmas behind OCD.
- **Find your voice:** Share your story in ways that make you feel comfortable. This could be your most powerful weapon against this stigma. Talk to someone you trust or an online support group or try to implement creative outlets like writing or art. Your experience can be a tool that could help someone else find their understanding.
- **Be vulnerable:** This is much like finding your voice, but here, you need to push past the fear of judgment. That fear keeps you isolated. Being vulnerable doesn't mean you're weak. This is one of the strongest things one can do to break down the walls.

- **Celebrate the wins:** Cheer yourself on because every small victory in this climb is something to celebrate. If you question your celebrations, remember that you're going against your own mind, which is an extremely powerful adversary.
- **Join a movement:** Remember that you aren't battling this all alone. You are part of a large community of us who are chasing the same goals as you. Look into supporting organizations like the OCD Foundation or National Alliance on Mental Illness (NAMI), participate in awareness campaigns, and just connect with those who are battling alongside you.

———

With that, we round out the first part of the journey. You should have a much better understanding of OCD and the basics of this debilitating disorder. Now we can move beyond the broad terms and the "we" and "us." We move on looking solely at the person that matters most in this—you. So let's shuffle into the next section and help you understand the ways that OCD shows up in *your* life, which will help you to gain better personal awareness.

MAGNIFYING THE SIGNS

"It's not the thoughts but rather what you do with them that maintains the OCD cycle."

— KATIE D'ATH AND ROB WILSON

In the first part of our journey, we got what could be described as a bird's eye view into the symptoms of this disorder, but now it's time to zoom in on it as we continue. Think of this chapter as an in-depth review, but remember to keep the focus on yourself. The goal here is to be able to see the signs of OCD in your own life, which will take us closer to managing those symptoms.

OCD SYMPTOMS: A DEEP DIVE

For this first section, we will look at the symptoms of OCD. These are going to include the physical and psychological signs. As you read through, try to do a physical and mental scan to see if you are familiar with any of them and maybe trace back to when you first noticed them.

Physical Signs of OCD

While we understand that OCD is a battle that's taking place in the mind, its stranglehold on us goes well beyond anxious thoughts and intrusive urges. The way OCD manifests itself physically can be just as disruptive to our lives, and it only adds another layer to the already complex web.

Your body speaks to you, and one of the ways it does is through hyperawareness. This makes everyday sensations become an intrusive signal. Because the brain is stuck in a hyper-focus, it can lead to physical discomfort and leave you exhausted. There are also movements driven by compulsion, which are actions like handwashing, going back and checking, or arranging. After enough time, the compulsive actions can become demanding, and it can lead to skin irritations, muscle fatigue, and even repetitive strain injuries. You can't ignore the stress response, either. The constant anxiety that is triggered by OCD can lead to symptoms like headaches, stomachaches, and trouble sleeping.

With a decent understanding of OCD and basic symptoms, you probably notice these immediately. However, your body can also speak through some hidden impacts; so let's look at a few of them.

- **Skin conditions:** If you excessively wash and clean, this can lead to dry, cracked skin, eczema, and even skin infections.
- **Digestive issues:** The chronic anxiety and stress that come with OCD can affect your digestive system, leaving you with issues like nausea, constipation, or diarrhea.

- **Sleep disruptions:** The intrusive thoughts, anxiety, and physical discomfort you feel can make it hard to fall asleep and stay asleep. There could even be bouts of insomnia, which further impacts physical well-being.

Psychological Signs of OCD

Now we can step past the rituals and compulsive physical behaviors that come with OCD. This disorder is a complex realm filled with psychological distress. The unwanted thoughts will take precedence, and that will fuel your anxiety and fear. Therefore, let's look into and see if you can identify any of these psychological signs.

The most obvious psychological sign of OCD is what we can dub "the vortex."

- The vortex starts with the unrelenting, disturbing thoughts that fill your daily life. These are the obsessions that we have already gone over.
- The vortex then gets its power when the brain struggles to let go of the thoughts. They simply repeat, and any attempt to quiet them down is futile and only fuels further anxiety.
- The rest of the vortex's power occurs because while you realize that the obsessive thoughts you have are irrational, there is such a strong emotional pull toward the obsessions that you're just caught in the cycle.

Much like compulsions, our obsessions have deeper connections and might leave you in a state of emotional torment.

- **Anxiety:** You have seen this one before, but it is the most prevalent issue. Obsessions trigger intense anxiety, which makes it difficult to function normally. Your work, relationships, and other aspects of daily life are overshadowed by intrusive thoughts.

- **Shame and isolation:** There is a stigma around mental health, where you could feel like you're wrong or broken for having OCD. This shame could be causing you to withdraw from social interactions because you fear judgment from those around you.
- **Exhaustion:** This can lead to a higher level of exhaustion.

WHAT ARE COMPULSIONS?

As we mentioned early on, when you have these obsessions, the only way you know to cope with them is through compulsions. So let's peel back the layers a bit more on what compulsions are and if they are causing you harm.

Defining Compulsions

Compulsions are just the repetitive behaviors or mental acts that you do as you try to lessen the anxiety that is caused by your obsession. It's like a pressure valve—while it can offer some relief, it isn't a permanent solution. For example, the person who washes their hands repeatedly is trying to silence their fear of germs. However, they are aware that their hands and area are clean.

Signs of a Compulsion

The real sign is with repetition or excess. Let's use hand washing, again, as an example. Doing this once after using the restroom is normal, but when you have to do it multiple times in a row because of the intrusive thought of germs—that's a sign of compulsion.

Remember, our compulsions are driven by the need to lessen the anxiety we feel thanks to an obsession. Someone who has anxiety about losing their keys will lock themselves in a ritual of checking their pockets or bag multiple times, even when they know where their keys are.

Another thing that will set things apart is that compulsions are irresistible. It's like there is something in your head that makes you give in because you want to avoid the anxiety.

How Compulsions Are Harmful

Compulsions aren't necessarily dangerous. Even those who have thoughts of violence rarely act on them; however, they can have a severe impact on your daily life.

- **Time-consuming:** Your rituals can eat up a huge chunk of time, which can lead to impacts on your professional life, relationships, and downtime.
- **Isolation:** The fear of being judged for your compulsion can lead to withdrawal from social activities.
- **Distress and exhaustion:** The vortex of OCD is mentally and emotionally draining.
- **Interferes with life:** Compulsion can become so dominant for some that it prevents them from even engaging in normal tasks, let alone the things they *want* to do.

Again, those aspects alone don't make compulsions harmful, but they can trigger more issues like increased anxiety, depression, and other issues. That's where a person with OCD can start traveling down a dark path.

IDENTIFYING INTRUSIVE THOUGHTS

Imagine a thought popping into your head, one that is unwelcome and unwanted. This could be something like a violent image, a blasphemous idea, or it could be a distressing doubt about yourself or someone close to you. This is an intrusive thought, and they are the very things that lead to distress and anxiety. Sometimes, these thoughts are mistaken as normal, which means we need to learn how to recognize these unwanted guests. This is how you will take a much bigger step toward managing your thoughts and regaining your peace of mind.

What are Intrusive Thoughts?

Unlike your normal thoughts, which flow naturally, intrusive thoughts are any thoughts that are involuntary, unwanted, and cause a great deal of distress. We've seen this before but let's review the different forms intrusive thoughts can take.

- **Violent or aggressive:** These thoughts are often mental images of harming yourself or others, even those whom you care a lot about.
- **Sexual in nature:** Having unwanted, disturbing, or inappropriate thoughts of a sexual nature is intrusive.
- **Faith-based or blasphemous:** If you are a spiritual person, these thoughts can be doubts about your faith, or they can be intrusive, sacrilegious ideas.
- **Contamination related:** This one, we know, is the fear of germs, dirt, or the spread of illness.
- **Doubts and worries:** These intrusive thoughts can be about your relationships, financial problems, or even your health concerns.

These thoughts can often feel unreal and irrational, and they can be severely off-putting to you. However, despite feeling disconcerted, the thoughts will persist. They will also be joined by feelings like intense anxiety and a desperate urge to silence them.

How to Identify Intrusive Thoughts

One thing that concerns those with OCD is trying to discern if a thought is intrusive or if it is just a fleeting thing that happens from time to time. The following are just some clues that can help you spot the difference.

- **Unwanted and upsetting:** Do you try to make the thought go away because it feels disturbing or wrong?
- **Repetitive and persistent:** Does the intrusive thought keep repeating itself, even when you attempt to ignore it?
- **Anxiety and distress:** When the thought comes through, does it trigger feelings of fear, shame, or guilt?
- **Feels out of character:** Does the thought go against your morals, values, or beliefs?

What is important to remember about intrusive thoughts is that it's normal to have them on occasion. Therefore, one intrusive thought isn't cause for alarm. It's the intensity, frequency, and emotional distress you feel that separates a regular thought from an intrusive one.

RECOGNIZING YOUR TRIGGERS

I want to pass down an example I heard when I started my own climb against OCD. Imagine that you're walking through a peaceful setting. It can be a meadow, the woods, or just the block around your home, but now imagine that this setting is littered with landmines.

Every step that you take could potentially set off an explosion. That explosion is one of anxiety, fear, and the unmistakable urge to just flee, and once that landmine goes off, it's like a chain reaction.

This is how it feels for us living with OCD. In this world, the most ordinary sights, sounds, and even emotions can be a triggered landmine. Once it goes off, it sets off a chain reaction of intrusive thoughts followed by the desperate need to engage in our compulsions.

What Are Triggers?

This brings us to our triggers, the ones that are specifically in the context of OCD. What causes us to have intrusive thoughts, which then lead to our compulsions?

Our triggers are specific internal or external stimulants that activate obsessive thoughts and compulsions. And as you've learned before, triggers vary between each person dealing with this disorder. So, let's get a much closer look at potential triggers.

- **Environmental:** Your triggers can come from certain places or objects around you. Even seeing numbers can trigger intrusive thoughts and compulsions. For example, someone with contamination fears could be set off at the sight of dirty dishes. Meanwhile, someone with obsessions with order and symmetry will be triggered when seeing an object unevenly placed or disordered.
- **Emotional:** Our triggers can also live in emotions like stress, anxiety, sadness, and even happiness. The compulsions typically come when we feel overstimulated; so difficult life events, relationship issues, and even exciting news can be a landmine of intrusive thoughts.

- **Physical:** Things like fatigue and hunger can act as triggers. Even sensations like a racing heart or sweaty palms can set someone down the path toward their compulsions.
- **Cognitive:** Certain thoughts, memories, and even internal dialogues can bring up OCD symptoms. Those who have harm-based OCD will be triggered by intrusive thoughts about violence. There are also those moments where you could be triggered by a specific memory.

How to Identify Triggers

Identifying your personal triggers is a monumental step in getting your OCD under control. I do have to say, though, that this is going to be a challenging process. However, by staying the course, you can start defusing the hidden landmines. That will prevent them from taking control of your life. The following are some solid ways you can begin identifying your triggers.

- **Keep a journal:** Keep track of your thoughts, feelings, and behaviors throughout a typical day. Note any situations, emotions, or experiences that come right before a flood of intrusive thoughts. As time goes on, this might help you pick up on patterns, which will reveal your potential triggers.
- **Use mindful observation:** Pay attention to your environment when you have OCD symptoms. This includes your internal environment along with the external one. When this happens, ask yourself questions like, "What was I thinking or feeling before I got the intrusive thoughts?" or "What was happening around me? What was I doing?" Asking yourself these types of

questions can help you identify triggers that might have
been long overlooked.

- **Utilize professional guidance:** Working with someone
  like a counselor or a therapist who specializes in OCD can
  be a tool for those who severely struggle with the disorder.
  These professionals will help you identify and understand
  your triggers in a safe environment, and they can support
  you as you find treatment.

By getting to this point, you already deserve a huge congratula-
tions! Unmasking the symptoms of OCD is a great marker to
reach on this climb. By knowing the symptoms and what impact
this disorder has on your life, you can start chipping away and
finding the right treatment for yourself.

But we have not reached the summit yet. Now, we get to gear up
and consider the next crucial step: professional diagnosis. Why?
Because, in many instances, this is a disorder that you can't battle
on your own. Also, a diagnosis is going to give you specialized
support, the kind that you deserve. Think therapy and specific
treatment plans. It's this kind of help that will empower you to
manage your OCD effectively, and it makes a lot of the things in
this book far more effective.

This is a powerful move toward reclaiming control; so if you're
ready, I'll show you how.

INTO THE DOCTOR'S OFFICE

"It's like a broken machine. Thoughts go in your head, get stuck, and keep going around and around."

— MEGAN FLYNN

Walking into a doctor's office armed with your symptoms and preliminary explanations as to why you think you have OCD (or any disorder) can be nothing short of awkward. Sometimes, it can even be a little nerve-racking, especially once they take you in. You start to wonder what they're looking for. You might even start to panic that you've gotten the whole thing wrong! Knowing what takes place during a diagnosis can ease a lot of that anxiety, and it can allow you to be properly prepared, which only helps you get a more accurate diagnosis. This chapter is aimed at making one of your biggest steps seem far less daunting of a task.

DIAGNOSTIC CRITERIA

If you've ever been on a walk in a new neighborhood, you're met with a lot of twists and turns, and you're unsure of where you really want to go. Diagnosing OCD can feel like the same journey, and that's largely because of how the symptoms all fall into this massive, tangled web. But that's where universal diagnostic criteria can come in and act like a compass, guiding you toward the clarity and support that you actually need.

The Foundation

At the heart of your diagnosis is the Diagnostic and Statistical Manual of Mental Disorders (DSM-5). It is a reference guide used by professionals that outlines specific criteria to help them issue a diagnosis. This is where gaining more knowledge about yourself and what OCD is can be extremely helpful.

Key Criteria

The things that they are going to look for are the presence of either obsessions or compulsions or both. This is why it is so important for you to know what these things are before stepping foot into a doctor's office. So, again, let's look at them.

- **Obsessions:** They will ask you if you have any intrusive and unwanted thoughts, urges, or images that cause you significant distress. Stay calm and remember that these intrusions are repetitive, persistent, and impossible to control.
- **Compulsions:** After they ask you about your thoughts, they will move on to determine if you have compulsions. What they are looking for are the actions and behaviors

that you use in an attempt to alleviate your anxiety or distress.

Beyond the Basics

While they are looking for the presence of obsessions and compulsions, they will also be looking beyond that; therefore, you should be prepared to get a little more in-depth with your answers. Don't worry, we will prepare you for the things they'll look for.

- **Time commitment:** Remember, your obsessions and compulsions are going to drain a lot of your time. What they are looking for is if these issues take more than one hour each day to complete.
- **Distress and impairment:** The symptoms you have should cause you clinically significant distress or debilitations in social, professional, and other important areas of your life. Occasional intrusions, anxieties, or rituals won't warrant a diagnosis, especially if your daily life isn't being disrupted.
- **Not substance-induced:** What they are looking for here is that your obsessions and compulsions aren't being caused by substance use or another type of medical condition. Those with severe allergies often find themselves cleaning in the same manner as someone with OCD.

Putting the Pieces Together

What you've been through is only part of the clinical evaluation that they will take. The professional will also need to observe your interactions and daily routine. While this is going to seem like a lot, you have to remember that getting a diagnosis (or no diagnosis) is going to turn you the way you need to go. It can give you access to the appropriate treatment, and it can empower you and give you a better understanding of your own thoughts and feelings (as well as the condition itself).

The important thing is to not see the professional as someone scary. They are experts and far better guides on your climb up this mountain. Now that you know the basics, we can really open up and dive into the diagnosis process.

THE DIAGNOSTIC PROCESS

Stepping into a doctor's office with the inkling that you have OCD is going to feel like a large leap. Even after knowing the things they will be looking for, it's still a doctor's office, and many of us still associate these places with a myriad of anxious triggers just waiting for us.

However, knowing the twists and turns of this process (in full detail) can give you the confidence that you need to keep your focus on what's important. Now, let's dive in and demystify the maze of the diagnostic process.

Diagnostic Tests and Screenings

You don't need to worry about a blood test or scan to find OCD, but your mental health professional is going to employ a few different tools that will not just give you a diagnosis but will also give you a clear picture of what you're going through. So let's look at some of those tools of the trade.

- **Clinical interview:** This involves an in-depth conversation, which is going to navigate through your symptoms, the timeline of your symptoms, the severity, and how it has impacted your life. Brace yourself, as you'll need to be open about your obsessions, compulsions, triggers, and any other mental health conditions. Being as open and honest as you can be is going to be the key because your doctor will need them to tailor your diagnosis.

- **Diagnostic scales and questionnaires:** Your doctor can implement standardized questionnaires including the Yale-Brown Obsessive Compulsive Scale or the National Institute of Mental Health's Diagnostic Interview for Genetic Studies (DIS-GS). These are like the clinical interviews, except they will be a little more structured. They help determine how severe your OCD is, and they can help separate it from any other mental health conditions.
- **Mental status examination:** This assessment is used to evaluate your overall mental state. It will look into your mood, thought patterns, and cognitive abilities. Like the questionnaires, this helps to ensure that your diagnosis is accurate while eliminating other potential explanations.

Step-by-Step Insights

Now that you know about the tools, let's dive in and go through each step that will be waiting for you.

1. **Initial consultation:** The starting line is a discussion of your concerns with your doctor or a mental health professional. Be ready to openly describe your symptoms and the impact they have on your life.
2. **Clinical interview and assessments:** After your consultation, the professional will probably conduct a thorough interview as we discussed in the last section. This is probably going to take more than one session, and

this is because they are trying to get the clearest picture of what you're going through.

3. **Differential diagnosis:** Your doctor is going to take some time and carefully consider if there are any other explanations for what you're experiencing, like anxiety disorders, trauma, or depression. You'll need to be patient through this because they need this time to ensure they are giving you an accurate diagnosis and the right treatment for it.

4. **Diagnosis and treatment plan:** Based on the information and their assessment of you, your doctor will come to your diagnosis and find a treatment plan that works for you. This can include therapy, medication, or both.

5. **Ongoing monitoring and adjusting:** Keep in mind that your diagnosis isn't a one-time thing. Your doctor will look at your progress regularly, and they will adjust as time goes on. This is done to make sure your treatment is successful.

Also, remember that this is not all on your doctor. This is a collaborative effort; so ask questions, clear up any doubts, and express your concerns. You should be a huge part of your mental health journey.

WHO CAN DIAGNOSE?

The path toward a diagnosis is an overwhelming one, even when you understand OCD and its symptoms. You aren't the only one who feels that way, but as overwhelming as it is, you have to find the right person to diagnose it. This is crucial because it's what will set you up with effective treatment.

So who should you turn to for a reliable diagnosis? Let's find the right people.

- **Licensed psychologists and psychiatrists:** These are mental health professionals with doctoral degrees, and they have had years of extensive training in diagnosing and treating all types of mental health conditions. They have all the tools to conduct a thorough evaluation, including using interviews, questionnaires, and other clinical observations to give you the best assessment of your symptoms. For the most accurate diagnosis and treatment plan, they should be your first choice.
- **Clinical social workers and licensed mental health counselors:** These professionals will typically have master's degrees, and they have also gotten specialized training in counseling and therapy regarding mental health. They don't have the same level of diagnostic authority as psychologists and psychiatrists, but they still play a huge role in the process. Because of their training, they will likely refer you to someone else to get a formal diagnosis. They are great at getting valuable support and guidance.
- **General practitioners:** Your primary care physician isn't a specialist in mental health, but they can be a great first point of contact. They can screen you for OCD symptoms, and they can refer you to a mental health professional.

It is important to remember that not everyone can give you an OCD diagnosis, and one of those people is you. Do not rely on online quizzes, self-diagnosis, or advice from someone who isn't a trained mental health professional. They are not accurate and cannot give you the treatment you need.

It also needs to be said that finding the right professional is a tall mountain to climb. So again, let's dive in to help you navigate this part of the journey.

SEEKING PROFESSIONAL HELP

Now that you know what to expect and who can give you the diagnosis and the treatment that you need to battle this disorder, you need to know where to look. There are a lot of avenues out there that you can take, which makes it seem daunting. However, we will peel back those layers so you can find not just the right kind of help but the right fit for you. We will also look at some of the red flags that you should look for when seeking help.

Where to Seek Professional Help

Let's start with where you can turn to find the right kind of help since there is more than one way to get there.

- **Specialized resources:** Organizations like the International OCD Foundation (IOCDF) will give you several resources to find therapists and treatment centers that specialize in OCD. You can use their searchable directory to find locations, insurance providers, and even treatment approaches, which can narrow your options to meet your needs without breaking your budget.
- **Local mental health networks:** You can always use your primary care physician or your local mental health clinic. These can provide you with referrals to qualified professionals near you.
- **Teletherapy options:** For those who are concerned about accessibility, you can implement online platforms like Talk space or Better Help, which can connect you in a video

conference with a licensed therapist who specializes in OCD.

Now that you have an idea of the therapists around you, it's time to schedule consultations to get a feel for how they approach these issues and to see if their personality fits with yours.

- **Expertise in OCD:** Your therapist needs to have experience and training with OCD. Certifications like Certified CBT Therapist (CBT-T) or exposure and response prevention (ERP) training are things that should stand out to you.
- **Collaborative approach:** Therapy needs to feel like a partnership. It's not all up to you or your therapist. You should feel heard, understood, and that you are part of the decision-making process.
- **Compassion and empathy:** You want a therapist who creates a safe and supportive space where you feel like you can be vulnerable and openly express your concerns.
- **Realistic expectations:** Discuss what approach they take to your treatment, how long it will take, and any challenges that may come up. This is a journey, so be wary of anyone saying that they can expedite your treatment.

Common Therapy Red Flags

That brings us to the red flags of therapy. Just to ease your mind, most therapists are dedicated professionals who care about your betterment. However, some people have had less-than-ideal experiences with "professionals." Here's a list of red flags that you should check for, and if you see them, then find someone else immediately.

- **Dismissiveness or lack of understanding:** Any concerns and experiences that you have should be taken seriously. If your therapist is minimizing your struggles, showing skepticism about OCD, or making you feel invalidated, then you should reconsider having them treat you.
- **Unprofessional behavior:** Your therapist should *never* make inappropriate jokes or judgmental comments. They should also not breach confidentiality in any way. These behaviors are unacceptable.
- **Pressure to conform:** A true professional will look for treatments meant for you. If they are trying to push you into a treatment because "it's worked for other people," then they aren't approaching you with your best interests at heart.
- **Lack of progress or unclear communication:** If you've been in several sessions and feel stuck or confused as to what you're supposed to be doing, or if your therapist is vague about everything, you need to consider a second opinion.

This is an investment in your mental well-being, not to mention your money, so do not settle for less-than-optimal treatment.

Knowing what to expect when choosing your professional help and what to expect when you head in for your evaluation can make the process a much less daunting task. But what are they going to tell you when it comes to options regarding your treatment? Not knowing what to expect when it comes to the specific treatment for your OCD can cause the anxiety to ramp up yet again, so in the next chapter, we will spend some time exploring those options.

WHAT ARE MY OPTIONS?

"At its crux, OCD treatment is about learning to live with the discomfort of uncertainty."

— JEFF BELL

Of course, it's more than just getting into the doctor's office and getting a proper diagnosis. The next part of this climb is your treatment. OCD has innumerable treatment options that you will be given the option to explore. As we close the second summit of our climb, we will look at the professional and holistic treatment options out there that could potentially ease the effects of your OCD.

Just a word of caution before we continue. It's crucial to get guidance before implementing any tools to help your OCD. This information is meant to be empowering to your journey, but self-directed treatment can be risky as it can make your OCD symptoms worse.

COGNITIVE-BEHAVIORAL THERAPY

In the battle against a lot of mental health issues, including OCD, cognitive-behavioral therapy (CBT) is one of the most powerful allies. But you might be wondering just what exactly this approach is and how it can help you navigate your own maze of obsessions and compulsions.

What Is CBT?

CBT is a collaborative therapy effort between you and your therapist. The focus here is on identifying and then challenging the unwanted thought patterns and behaviors that cause your OCD to thrive. Think of it as a way to rewire those threads in your mind. You'll gradually replace the anxiety-inducing obsessions with realistic and empowering thoughts.

To get a better understanding of CBT, we will look at what happens in a typical therapy session for those with OCD.

- **Understanding the OCD cycle:** You'll explore the cycle of OCD, which means you and your therapist will spend time identifying your specific triggers, obsessions, and compulsions. This is where you'll get your treatment roadmap.
- **Cognitive restructuring:** This stage is important as you'll learn to examine if your intrusive thoughts are valid. You'll recognize the distorted thinking patterns, and by analyzing those thoughts, you will get the power to really challenge them and their legitimacy. This is how you will begin to reduce the impact of those thoughts.
- **Exposure and response prevention:** This is the core component of CBT, and it involves gradually exposing

yourself to the things that trigger your OCD. This is done in a safe and controlled manner, and it will help you learn to resist your compulsion urges. This will help you break down the fear and anxiety that are associated with your triggers.

- **Developing healthy coping mechanisms:** CBT will give you the practical tools to take on your anxiety and distress. Your therapist will give you ideas like relaxation techniques, mindfulness exercises, and healthy habits that will allow you to manage your emotions and compulsions in a much healthier way and not allow them to take over.

Where to Find CBT?

As we learned in the last chapter, you need to find a therapist who has training in OCD, but now, you should look for one who has training in CBT, too. There are a few resources that I'll list below.

- International OCD Foundation (iocdf.org)
- Anxiety and Depression Association of America (adaa.org)
- Psychology Today therapist directory (psychologytoday.com/us)
- University-based CBT clinics: If there are any universities near you, they potentially have CBT services, and you can get them at a reduced rate. These are perfect if you are on a budget or want to try CBT for a bit before making a full commitment.

Is Self-Guided CBT Effective?

Again, professional guidance should be your ideal method when using CBT, but self-guided CBT (self-treatment) is a valuable tool for you, especially if you have limited access to your therapist. In many cases, those who are committed to their betterment can see significant progress when using self-guided CBT.

While you should gain some guidance from a professional, the following are some effective tools that you can use for self-guided CBT.

- **CBT workbooks and online programs:** Several programs and other books will help you. The only challenge is making sure the resources you use are reputable. This means that you will need to do your research and read reviews.
- **Journaling and self-monitoring:** Keeping track of your thoughts, feelings, and compulsions can help you zero in on your patterns and triggers, which is very helpful as you get assistance.
- **Exposure and response prevention exercises:** Again, while you can do this one on your own, be aware that this is aimed at setting off your compulsions. You will gradually expose yourself to your triggers, and as you do, you will practice resisting your compulsions. This can be a very effective method as long as you stay committed to the process.
- **Mindfulness and relaxation techniques:** You can employ techniques like deep breathing or meditation. These can reduce distress and allow you to avoid relying on your compulsions.

Again, self-guided CBT requires dedication and consistency. If you're struggling or your obsessions get worse, then you need to stop self-treatment and contact a professional.

Also, keep in mind that CBT might not be the fix that you need to overcome your OCD, but it will give you a much clearer roadmap.

When you use CBT, remember that you're going to need commitment, consistent participation, and a solid support system.

MEDICATION MANAGEMENT

Therapy is one of the best ways to alleviate the issues associated with OCD, but oftentimes, your therapist will prescribe medication, which will be another valuable companion on this climb. In this section, I will go through some of the most commonly prescribed medications used for OCD. This is aimed to take off some of the anxiety that is associated with medications.

Medication Types and What They Do

For this, we will look at the different types of medications and what they do, and then we will go just a bit further by looking at the names of these medicines, making it less scary if they are prescribed to you.

- **Selective serotonin reuptake inhibitors (SSRIs):** These medications are usually the go-to meds to deal with OCD symptoms, and they work by increasing your brain's serotonin levels. The most common are fluoxetine (Prozac), sertraline (Zoloft), and fluvoxamine (Luvox). Of the three types, fluvoxamine is an OCD-specific SSRI (IOCDF 2010c).
- **Serotonin-norepinephrine reuptake inhibitors (SNRIs):** These medications affect both serotonin and norepinephrine, which can provide some people with additional benefits. The most common SNRI is venlafaxine (Effexor) (IOCDF 2010c).
- **Tricyclic antidepressants (TCAs):** Most professionals are more inclined to go with SSRIs for OCD treatment;

however, something like clomipramine (Anafranil) would be up for consideration if you haven't responded well to other medications (IOCDF 2010c).

Now that we know *what* medications are presented in the battle against OCD, we can look at how these medications function concerning OCD.

- **Neurotransmitter regulation:** Let's start with SSRIs. These medications aim to work by increasing the available amount of serotonin in your body, which is a neurotransmitter that plays a key part in regulating your mood, anxiety, and obsessions. SNRIs, on the other hand, will do that while additionally impacting norepinephrine, which will further enhance your mood and emotional regulation (IOCDF 2010c).
- **Reduction of anxiety and obsessions:** By stabilizing your neurotransmitters, you will start to feel alleviated from the intense anxiety and intrusive thoughts that have been haunting you this long (IOCDF 2010c).
- **Curbing compulsive behaviors:** We are usually so focused on these medications working on our anxiety and obsessions, but we forget that the calm feeling we have afterward will actually help reduce our urges to engage in our compulsions (IOCDF, 2010c).

In a lot of cases, medication and therapy are an effective one-two punch, but there are some concerns when considering medication.

- Medication alone isn't the answer. You should still be active with your therapy sessions. To achieve that feeling of being free is going to take time and consistent effort.

- One of the reasons that this takes time is that you will need to work with your therapist to find the right dosage for you. Everyone is different, so you could need a lighter dose while someone else needs more to see any effect.
- Like any medication, there are side effects. These will vary, and sometimes they will be mild and will pass with time. But this means that you need to openly communicate with your therapist at all times about your concerns, side effects, and your experience while on the medication. Also, *never* adjust your dosage without talking to them first.
- You also have to think about how your body is going to react during the initial stages. Because these medications are working with your brain function, you could experience severe side effects. While only a small number of people experience suicidal thoughts when they first get on these medications, it is still a possibility. Again, maintain openness with your therapist when using medication.

In short, there are a lot of medications out there, and overall, they are generally safe. However, that safety is only guaranteed if you follow your therapist's instructions and maintain an open line of communication with them, especially when you first get on the medication. When used correctly, and by being consistent with your therapy, you have a pathway to the top of this mountain.

ALTERNATIVE AND COMPLEMENTARY THERAPIES

The first places that you want to look are always going to be traditional therapy and medication. These are the cornerstones of treatment; however, there are people out there who have found peace and comfort through a wide array of holistic approaches.

There are also several who use those alternates as complementary approaches.

With that said, using these approaches in conjunction with therapy and medication can be extremely powerful. They encourage you to manage your OCD symptoms, and they also encourage an increase in your overall well-being. I would still recommend discussing these approaches with your therapist or counselor before implementing them but let's look at these alternatives and see if any would be right for you.

Connecting to the Power of Nature

These simple things can go a long way in how your body functions, which can influence how your mind works.

- **Mindfulness and meditation:** Something like mindfulness meditation or even yoga can be tools to train the mind to be more aware of your intrusive thoughts and anxieties. They can also train your mind to be less reactive to those thoughts. When you can ground yourself in the present and focus on inner peace, you will be gaining the tools to help break the cycle of obsessions and compulsions.
- **Nutritional tweaks:** There is a strong belief that your diet can affect your mental health. Focusing your diet on fruits, vegetables, whole grains, and lean proteins will be great for your physical health, which will translate to your mental health. If you are looking for specific types of food that could potentially help you and your OCD, aim for ones that contain B12 and omega-3 fatty acids. It's also important to implement any changes carefully to avoid adverse reactions.

- **Herbal remedies:** There are some herbs like St. John's wort and passionflower that have been used by people to handle anxiety or mood disorders. They might provide some relief to your OCD symptoms, but because they are not scientifically tested treatments, results are going to vary greatly from person to person.

Movement and Embodiment

Again, while nothing is proven to naturally treat obsessive-compulsive disorder, we can't deny that when we get up and move around, we tend to feel better about a lot of things. So let's look at two aspects that might give you mental benefits and will certainly give you physical benefits.

- **Exercise and physical activity:** Getting up and regularly engaging in physical activity releases natural mood boosters known as endorphins. These endorphins can help combat stress and anxiety, which are heavily linked to OCD. Exercise also helps your ability to fall asleep and stay asleep. Improved sleep quality can also play a huge role in managing the symptoms of OCD. Maybe you have activities now that you enjoy or can think of some that pique your interest, so get out there and get moving.
- **Deep breathing and relaxation techniques:** Breathing techniques like diaphragmatic breathing or progressive muscle relaxation can help lower your heart rate and trigger the relaxation response in your body. Those relaxed feelings can be extremely helpful in managing the spikes in stress and anxiety that are caused by triggering thoughts or situations.

Creativity and Developing a Network

To close off the alternative methods of battling your OCD, we turn to our creativity and those around us. Sometimes, just getting these thoughts and feelings out of our heads and into another place can be just as beneficial as diet and exercise.

- **Art therapy and journaling:** Getting your thoughts and feelings out through art, music, or writing can make for a significant breakthrough in your self-exploration, and it can provide you with a different type of emotional release. These avenues will let you gain a deeper insight into your triggers and what you use to cope with them, which can promote self-compassion and acceptance.
- **Support groups and community:** Building a personal network and connecting with other people who understand the challenges that OCD can present can be not only validating but empowering, too. There might be support groups near you, or you can opt for an online community. Both of these are going to offer you a comforting environment to share your experiences, learn from each other, and develop a support system filled with encouragement and understanding.

What to Remember about These Approaches

Always remember that holistic and complementary treatments do not replace the traditional, effective ones. This is largely because these approaches have so much variation in effectiveness. These alternative routes need to be used in conjunction with your therapy and medication, so always consult with your healthcare professional.

Again, there is so much variation with these approaches. You and someone else could have the same type of OCD, the same triggers, and so on; however, you will both likely have vastly different results using these approaches. With that in mind, be patient and explore the different options until you find what clicks for you and works alongside your existing treatment.

And, to say it simply, do your best to stay safe and avoid unnecessary risks. Consult with your doctor or therapist before using an alternative approach.

Ah, that's better! We have reached another checkpoint, and now you know what to expect when it comes to your treatment. Over the last three chapters, you've taken in and mastered a lot when it comes to OCD. So now, it is time to focus on the things you can do to really help yourself along this process of recovery.

EXPOSURE AND RESPONSE PREVENTION

"You don't have to control your thoughts, you just have to stop letting them control you."

— DAN MILLMAN

You are now standing face-to-face with your deepest anxieties, intrusive thoughts, and triggers. All these things have brought you so much doubt and fear, but there is no turning back. You have to push forward and keep facing them.

This is the essence of exposure and response prevention (ERP), which is actually a very powerful tool when battling OCD. Now, its name might make you think that this is a forced confrontation and that you're going to be overwhelmed by anxiety, but we are here to unmask ERP. When you can understand its inner workings and why it's as effective as it is, you will then see that it can be a strong ally in managing your symptoms.

In this chapter, we will get into the science behind ERP, explore some unique techniques, and give you the knowledge that will help you easily take on this method of treatment.

WHAT ARE EXPOSURE THERAPY AND ERP?

Even if you've never been in a therapy session, you've likely heard how we should face our fears if we want to overcome something. That is exactly what we are going to do here, except there is an added layer that has shown itself to be more effective for OCD.

In this section, we will break down exposure therapy versus ERP, what it aims to do, and how it works.

What Is ERP?

Exposure and response prevention is a specialized method of CBT, and it's a groundbreaking approach for those who are battling OCD. It's like putting your OCD under a microscope because it exposes that intricate web made of your obsessions, compulsions, and anxiety. With ERP, you are facing your fears, but you are not just facing them; you are preventing your compulsive responses.

The exposure aspect of this involves you facing the things that trigger you head-on. This could be touching a doorknob for those with contamination fears, or it could be not looking at a setting and checking for symmetry if you have compulsions with the order of things. This is an intentional interaction with your triggers, and its purpose is to weaken the stimulation you feel when you are presented with these triggers.

Where ERP gets its magic, though, is in response prevention. This key element is the active resistance to give into the urge and engage in compulsions. Even when you feel anxiety, ERP will help you combat it. By not engaging in compulsions, your brain is forced to see the fear and learn that the triggers aren't as dangerous as they seemed.

ERP Versus Exposure Therapy

So we have ERP and exposure therapy, which both involve facing your fears. You might be wondering what the difference is. The key difference is in the approach to compulsions.

Exposure therapy zeroes in solely on facing your triggers; so your compulsions are left unaddressed. If you're combating other issues that involve triggers, like phobias, then exposure therapy alone can be helpful. However, when it comes to OCD, the cycle between your anxieties and compulsions remains, and that means the long-term success rate is much lower.

ERP, on the other hand, will show you that compulsions are also fueling the fires needed for your OCD to remain. When you actively prevent the behaviors, you disrupt that cycle. Therefore, your anxiety will decrease and the things that trigger you will lose their grip on you. Instead of just ignoring the problem, you are actively breaking it down piece by piece.

Goals of ERP

The biggest goal of ERP is to let you reclaim control of your life so you can live without being ruled by this disorder. But we can break that one large goal into a few smaller ones.

- **Reduce the frequency and intensity of obsessions and compulsions:** As you are slowly exposed to your OCD triggers and prevent your compulsive behavior, you are weakening the connections that ultimately make up the vicious OCD cycle.

- **Increase tolerance for anxiety:** When you can face anxiety without using your compulsions, you are building up your skills to face and manage your triggers in everyday situations.
- **Improve the quality of life:** ERP aims to break the cycle of OCD, which will then allow you to engage in activities and relationships that had once suffered because of the disorder.

How It Works

ERP is fascinating because it works in the realms of neuroscience and psychology. This brief explanation is just the bare bones of it, but it truly is a remarkable therapy method for anyone with OCD.

- **Habituation:** When you're repeatedly exposed to triggers while resisting your compulsions, you're weakening the fear response in your brain. The fear center of your brain uses this to learn that the feared stimuli aren't dangerous at all. This leads to a decrease in anxiety.
- **Extinction:** Remember, compulsions are temporary acts that reinforce our anxieties, but when you can prevent the behavior, you are ruining the cycle of reinforcement. This will break the connections that are in place between triggers and anxiety.

HOW SUCCESSFUL IS IT?

For those going through the brutal climb of the OCD mountain, ERP can feel like one of the most daunting climbs. It can be easy to fall into the thinking, *This isn't right for me,* but it always helps to take a breath and look at the stories of people who have used ERP and have found it to be an effective method. So, let's look at some of the triumphs and evidence that can help shine a light on this path.

ERP Success Stories

I have seen several success stories online, and I have encountered many who have benefited from ERP, so the stories here are brief and only two of the many I have witnessed.

- **Emily:** Emily had been long plagued by her fear of flying, although her job had her traveling frequently by plane. She developed elaborate rituals that all needed to be done or she would have even more debilitating anxiety entering the airport. After implementing ERP, she went through a series of small exposures, like visualizing the takeoff and even just booking a flight. The exposures progressed, and after each step, Emily found the courage to make these trips without all the rituals.
- **David:** David had a deep contamination obsession. It started with the surfaces outside of his home, but they eventually found their way in. His daily life was a battle, which led him to ERP. He confronted his fears head-on. He started with doorknobs and other small items, and eventually, he found that he was comfortable leaving his house without sanitizing everything he was going to touch. Now David has no problem with leaving his home and engaging in other activities.

These are only a couple of examples of people who have had success with ERP. Every story you may find on your own is going to be unique, but at the root of it is courage.

Studies on ERP

These stories are more than just anecdotes to give you hope; they stand hand-in-hand with extensive research that has looked into the effectiveness of ERP. Again, there is a lot of that research, so I'll just go over a few of them.

- A 2018 study gathered data from over 300 controlled trials. The selections were randomized, but the conclusion they came to was that ERP was far more effective at treating OCD than even the combination of medication and therapy.
- Another study done a year later, in 2019, followed OCD patients who had been using ERP for five years. Their results showed that these people had significant reductions in their OCD symptoms and general anxiety. The study also showed that the reductions were sustained, which showcased the long-term benefits of ERP.
- The last study that I will highlight investigated the brain changes that are associated with ERP. What it found was that the OCD patients on this treatment had increased brain activity in the regions that were in charge of emotional regulation, and there was less activity taking place in the fear center. This isn't definitive, but it does hint that ERP actually rewires the brain to manage anxiety more efficiently.

Sometimes, we just need to see proof. That proof usually comes through extensive studies, but it also comes from the people who used to struggle, just like we are, but found betterment through this method. From what we see here, ERP is much more than a promise; it is a powerful tool that can lead you to a significant change.

Now that we know this much about ERP, it's time to introduce you to what you can look forward to with this therapy, including how it can be done in a self-guided setting.

IMPLEMENTING ERP TECHNIQUES

So we know that ERP is effective and the basics of how it works, but now you are likely trying to discover what an ERP session looks like. What are the first steps of the journey? Can you do it alone? Of course, we are going to peel back the layers so you know what to expect when bringing ERP into your own therapy against OCD.

Typical ERP Session Experiences

Again, everything works much smoother and more effectively when you work with a therapist. Together, you will create a hierarchy of exposure. This is going to be like a step-by-step roadmap that lists and ranks your individual triggers. When you have that map, you're going to work in order from your least anxiety-provoking triggers to the most. For example, someone with contamination obsessions would touch a doorknob or other small surface to start the journey.

Your exposure might happen in real-life settings. For example, your therapist might have you venture into a lightly crowded space and build you up from there. In some cases, though, your exposure will be visualized from where your therapy sessions are taking place. As you move through this exposure, you'll learn how to resist the urge to use your compulsions.

The main thing that you need to keep in mind when going to ERP sessions is that these are a rollercoaster of emotions. You'll feel anxiety as you face your triggers, but with each successful section, those scared feelings will turn into ones of elation. When working with a therapist, you need to remember that it needs to be a collaborative effort. Your therapist needs to be your guide. They should be giving you support, encouragement, and training.

Self-Guided ERP

While I would still highly recommend doing this with a therapist, we have to understand that not everyone has access to professional therapy. There are even some who want to try it before they fully immerse themselves. Self-guided ERP is possible as long as you have a good sense of self-awareness and are careful during ERP. If your symptoms worsen during self-guided ERP, stop and consult a professional.

With that said, let's look at how you can practice on your own.

- **Create your exposure hierarchy:** Find your triggers and rank them from least to most anxiety-inducing. Do this because you will not find success starting with your biggest battles.
- **Plan your exposures:** Set aside dedicated time for these exercises. You want to make sure the environment is safe and controlled and that you are in the right headspace to practice.
- **Don't give into compulsions:** Your anxiety is going to rise, but you don't want to rely on the ritual that feeds into this cycle.
- **Find support:** Make sure you find an online community, people near you who have OCD, friends, family, podcasts, or anyone else who is going to provide you with a support system and ensure that you aren't battling alone.

Basic Exposure Therapy Steps

Before you take a deep dive into the realm of ERP, maybe you want to give yourself some basic exposure therapy as a way to prepare yourself. This is a much gentler approach, without putting focus on the compulsion aspect of your OCD. Again, if your symptoms get worse, stop using this and consult a professional.

- **Identify your fears:** Like you saw with ERP, the first thing you need to do is identify what sets your anxiety off. Be honest with yourself and list anything you can think of that adds to your OCD cycle.
- **Start with gradual exposure:** Never jump to your biggest fear. Start with the things that bring you mild anxiety. This is highly recommended when doing this by yourself to prevent magnifying your symptoms. Also, break your exposure down. For example, if you are afraid of dogs, then you would start by looking at pictures and working up from there.
- **Pay attention to your thoughts and feelings:** As you're working through your fears, observe your thoughts and emotions. You want to do this without judgment. Just observe. This stage is to get you to acknowledge that the negative feelings are there, but you aren't going to let them dictate your actions.
- **Reward yourself:** Even the smallest steps need to be celebrated. With where you have come from, completing an exposure exercise is a huge deal!

Again, self-guided ERP and basic exposure therapy practice need a level of caution. You also need to be gentle with yourself. If you aren't able to handle it on your own, this is not a bad thing. There are so many out there who need the support system of a professional in their corner.

"Exposure" sounds scary at first, but it's not as bad as your initial feelings told you it was. ERP can work wonders for your OCD, and exposure therapy is great if you have other fear triggers. However, let's look at the last couple of sections of this chapter. For some, there aren't a lot of options out there, and they can't get the help they need for several reasons. If that is you, then do not worry! Let's take a look at some other ways you can get relief from your OCD symptoms from the comfort of your home.

MINDFULNESS AND SELF-COMPASSION

"Recovery from OCD is possible. Keep fighting, keep pushing, and most importantly, keep believing in yourself."

— SHEILA MURRAY BETHEL

There are many who can't get into a professional setting for therapy. No matter the reason, I understand that it can be unfortunate. But remember, you are not alone in your battle, and while professional help is invaluable, there are still some powerful tools you can use. These tools don't need a doctor's office or the hefty price tag, and they will hold you over until you can find resources near you that will get you into that professional setting. With that, welcome to the world of mindfulness and self-compassion.

Often underrated, they can make a dynamic team when it comes to supporting your battle with OCD, which makes this the perfect addition. The goal here is to give you an understanding of what these techniques are and how they can be employed when it comes to healing OCD.

WHAT IS MINDFULNESS?

At the very core of mindfulness is the practice of paying attention to the present moment without being judgmental of it. You are stepping back and looking at all your thoughts and emotions with curiosity and acceptance. Basically, you are just letting things come as they are because you know that you can't change the moment, you can only react to it.

When it comes to a person and obsessive-compulsive disorder, the ability to observe thoughts and feelings without judgment is profound. The intrusive thoughts that are powered by our anxieties and fears typically feel like a command. They want us to act because they need their existence. However, mindfulness lets you see these thoughts as just something that passes through your brain. They are not something that needs to be handled in that instant. Instead, you are taking the time to step back and look at them, which oftentimes invalidates the thought.

By taking away the power that intrusive thoughts can have, mindfulness also works by taking away the need to use our compulsions. As you've learned previously, compulsions might be a reaction to your triggers, but they ultimately fuel the fire of your OCD. Mindfulness will let you *choose* a different response instead of being on autopilot.

Benefits

The benefits of mindfulness, especially when dealing with OCD, go far beyond just managing your symptoms. Here is a short list of the other ways this practice will benefit you.

- **Reduced anxiety and distress:** When you lower your reactions to intrusive thoughts, you are disrupting the cycle that comes from anxiety and compulsions. This eases your overall distress.
- **Improved emotional regulation:** When you can observe emotions without judging them, you will gradually find that you have the tools to manage them more effectively. It's a preventative measure against emotional surges.
- **Enhanced self-awareness:** Mindfulness will give you a deeper understanding of your thoughts, feelings, and even your bodily sensations. This allows you to have a better sense of inner clarity and control.
- **Increased acceptance:** When you're mindful, you can recognize the intrusive thoughts, but you are also not going to jump at the chance and use compulsions to quiet them down.
- **Relapse resilience:** When you practice mindfulness, you are strengthening your mental muscles, which makes you far more resilient when you are challenged in the future by OCD.

Mindfulness is a great tool that can calm a lot of anxieties, but you have to remember that, like with other treatments, this isn't a cure-all or a quick fix. Mindfulness requires regular practice, and you have to remain dedicated. However, if implemented correctly, you will have a very powerful ally against your OCD.

THE DEFINITION OF SELF-COMPASSION

When living with OCD, you are out of the present moment, and it can also make you look at yourself from a perspective of guilt and shame. You beat yourself up for having these intrusive thoughts and for using compulsions as a coping mechanism. But this is where self-compassion can turn the course with that thinking.

Self-compassion is the concept of treating yourself with the same kindness and understanding that you would give to a close friend or family member experiencing hardship. Self-compassion is about recognizing that we are all human, and humanity means that we have imperfections. This thinking then flows through and gives a gentle understanding of your struggles. Let's briefly look at the three pillars of this concept.

- **Mindfulness:** You can't reach a point of self-compassion without mindfulness. Remember that this means you recognize what is happening without judgment.
- **Common humanity:** This means that you understand that imperfections and struggles are all a part of every human life, not personal failures.
- **Self-kindness:** This is when you give yourself the same soothing words and actions that you would give a loved one in need.

Benefits

Practicing self-compassion can be a transformative practice, which means you're going to get plenty of benefits. Let's look at some of those in closer detail.

- **You'll break the cycle of shame:** This is an often-overlooked aspect of OCD, but the disorder often leaves the afflicted feeling shamed or inadequate. Self-compassion lets you see that the intrusive thoughts are only symptoms, not a reflection of your worth. As you loosen the grip of shame, you'll create a space for healing.

- **You'll reduce distress and anxiety:** As you know, your compulsions stem from your attempt to control your intrusive thoughts and anxieties. Self-compassion will help you accept these experiences, so you'll be able to observe them without getting lost in the shuffle. Over time, you'll see a decrease in overall distress, which will result in less need for compulsive behavior.
- **You'll build resilience:** When you tackle these challenges with self-compassion, your emotional strength will increase. You learn to get through these tough times with understanding and kindness, which gives you the tools needed to bounce back from any setbacks.
- **Your treatment outcomes will be enhanced:** When you can incorporate self-compassion into treatments like CBT and ERP, it can help you make significant improvements to their outcomes. When you double up your approach, you can manage your symptoms while building a sense of inner peace and self-acceptance.
- **You will foster self-acceptance:** A crucial aspect of living a meaningful life is to accept yourself and any flaws that may be present. Self-compassion allows you to embrace those imperfections, which then lets you display your true self and forge deeper connections with other people.

This also requires consistent effort and the willingness to be patient with yourself. Using things like mindful breathing, self-affirmations, and journaling can be the best ways to cultivate this tool.

Keep in mind that self-compassion is not just ignoring your struggles or thinking that harmful behaviors are okay. This is about being kind to yourself as you take on these challenges, just like you would with a loved one facing a tough time. This approach can be just what you need to get through the challenges of OCD with more resilience and more peace.

REDUCING ANXIETY THROUGH PRESENT MOMENT AWARENESS

Now that you are familiar with mindfulness, we can look at a few very specific techniques that you can use to implement it. Keep in mind that when you are mindful, you are not trying to ignore your anxieties. You are staying in the present moment and observing your anxieties with curiosity, and without judgment.

- **Use an anchoring practice:** When you start to feel your intrusive thoughts pulling you toward your compulsive habits, take some time to anchor yourself in the present by using your senses. This is a simple exercise that involves looking for five things you can see, four things you can touch, three things you can hear, two things you can smell, and one thing you can taste. This exercise forces your brain to be engaged in the present moment, which makes it hard for anxiety to take hold of you.
- **Use the power of your breath:** Your breath is there for you all the time, so let this constant companion be your anchor. Start by focusing on the sensation of your breath as it enters and leaves your body. You should feel the rise and fall of your chest. Then think about the cool air entering your nostrils and how it's warm as it exits. If your mind starts to wander back to your thoughts, then bring your attention back to your breath. This practice is aimed at calming your nervous system and brings a sense of inner peace.
- **Implement a body scan:** You will explore your body from just your thoughts, and pay attention to each part without

judgment. Start with your toes by wiggling them and take note of any sensations. From there, move your focus slowly up your legs, feeling any tension or relaxation in your muscles. Continue to your torso, arms, head, and everywhere else on your body where you'll observe any aches, tingling, or any feeling of being alive in your body. This practice is extremely helpful in bringing awareness to the present moment while detaching you from any intrusive thoughts you may have.

- **Use mindful observation:** When you have an intrusive thought, you should want to observe it with curiosity. You want to notice the content of the thought, the emotions you feel because of it, and then any bodily sensations it brings up. Do your best to avoid judgment and analysis, or try to ignore the thought. Your goal here is to just observe the thoughts while not giving in to them. Think of this as a way to weaken the power of intrusive thoughts.
- **Bring yourself to the center:** There is a slew of mental chatter in your mind, but there is still a place in you where peace resides. This is your center, and it will act as another anchor in the sea of intrusive thoughts. You can reach this place through practices like meditation. Find a comfortable, seated position and close your eyes. Start to focus on your breath, and as your intrusive thoughts come through, simply acknowledge them and return your focus back to your breath. This will take time, but eventually, you will find it easier to get to this quiet place when anxiety is triggered.

These methods are effective, but it's important to remember that there will be days when your thoughts can be overwhelming. That is okay. The important part of all this is to be gentle with yourself and try to keep bringing yourself back to a place of calm in the present moment.

CULTIVATING SELF-ACCEPTANCE WITH OCD

Living with OCD is hard because, before treatment, these intrusive thoughts and compulsions will make you feel like you're broken and just not good enough. You also blame yourself for having OCD, but as you learned in this chapter, self-compassion is just the tool you'll need to stop this cycle of negative thinking.

The following are some ways that you can cultivate more self-acceptance as you battle OCD.

- **Challenge your inner critic:** There's that little voice inside of you that loves to magnify all your flaws, and it filters in nothing but negativity. When it starts beating you down for engaging with your compulsions, this is when you need to practice gentle self-talk. Remember, OCD is a very intricate illness, not a reflection of failure on your part. Ask yourself if you would berate someone for their mental health issues, then question why your voice is trying to blame you.
- **Practice mindfulness:** Using one of the techniques that were listed above can help you recognize your thoughts and feelings without judgment. This means you can see that these are thoughts, not reflections of you as a person. It also means you accept them as thoughts and not absolute truths.
- **Accept imperfection:** This world is filled with an endless need for perfection, but trying to reach that point is exhausting and you'll never reach perfection. OCD often leaves you in a state of comparison and self-doubt. Instead,

embrace your imperfections because you're a unique human with your own amazing strengths.

- **Be kind to yourself:** Always treat yourself with the same compassion that you would treat someone else. When your thoughts are berating you, think about what you would say to your friend at that moment. Cheer yourself on, celebrate even the smallest of wins, and give yourself the encouragement to push on.

- **Learn to forgive yourself:** Mistakes will be made on your journey. There will be times when you unknowingly engage in a compulsion, and while this is a setback, it's all a part of the process. Don't dwell on what happened or on missed opportunities. Instead, use it as a learning experience and move forward.

- **Get support:** You shouldn't have to navigate your way through this all by yourself. Try connecting with others who have been a part of the journey or people still in it. You can do this in person or through online forums, but being able to share your experience and learn from others is empowering and validating. Building your own network will ensure that you don't have to tackle your toughest challenges alone.

OCD is a relentless storm, but you can face it head-on with mindfulness and self-compassion. While they aren't cure-alls, they can be great guides through some of the toughest times. The best part of these skills is that they aren't tied to therapy or schedules; they are flexible tools that you can use anywhere at any time. No matter where you find yourself, you won't have to feel alone with the intrusive thoughts that come with OCD.

OCD MANAGEMENT LIKE A PRO

"You are not your illness. You have an individual story to tell. You have a name, a history, a personality. Staying yourself is part of the battle."

— JULIAN SEIFTER

To finish off this part of your journey, we will take a deep dive into some final techniques, tips, and tricks that will help you along your journey. While they do not replace the effectiveness of therapy and medications, these will help you cope with triggers, understand your needs, and much more. These are the final layers of personal skills that will assist you in skillful OCD management.

COMMON COPING TECHNIQUES

Navigating the landscape of OCD can feel like a constant, steep climb. Intrusive thoughts cascade over your mind, and your anxieties surround you until you give in to your compulsions. Sometimes, when it feels like what you're trying isn't enough, some of these coping techniques may be able to help you. These tools have been honed by those who have navigated their own OCD, and now they are passed down to you.

Relaxation

- **Mindfulness:** You've already learned how mindfulness can steady your mind. Practice techniques like meditation and deep breathing, allowing you to objectively observe your thoughts and feelings. When you can keep your focus on the present moment, you break free from the grasp of your intrusive thoughts and find peace.
- **Progressive muscle relaxation:** Here, you tense and relax different muscle groups. When you release your muscle tension, this can have a calming effect on your nervous system. This will also take your focus away from the intrusive thought, placing it on the group of muscles that you're tensing up.
- **Yoga and tai chi:** These practices combine your physical movement with mindfulness, which is great for increasing your physical and mental health. As you move through the gentle flow of postures and poses, you focus on your breath, which can calm your anxieties and bring you a sense of balance.

Stress Reduction

- **Regular exercise:** Physical activity is one of the best relievers of stress. Take part in doing things that you enjoy, like walking, swimming, dancing, or anything that gets you moving. You will be releasing endorphins, which are those mood boosters that will help you work through your most anxious moments.

- **Good sleep habits:** Develop a consistent sleep schedule, because being rested is a crucial component when managing stress. To ensure you're getting a good night's sleep, create a bedtime routine, maintain a relaxing sleep environment, and try to avoid screen time before sleep.
- **CBT:** You learned earlier what CBT is and how it has the studies to back it up. Challenging your anxious thoughts will leave you with plenty of room to restructure them. When you know that a thought is only a thought, you will gain control over your emotional response and how you handle stress.

Intentional Distractions

- **Do things you enjoy:** One of the best distractions from your anxious thoughts is usually through hobbies and activities that you find fulfilling. Whether you listen to music, read a book, or just spend some time walking outside, these things will keep your mind off your intrusive thoughts and anxiety.
- **Take on a challenge:** Use the time to learn a new skill or take on a project that you've had on your list. The focus you have to put into this activity will push the intrusive thoughts you have to the side. Besides forgetting the intrusions, you will feel accomplished because you've conquered a new challenge.
- **Socialize and connect:** Spending your time with friends and family can be a great escape from the isolation that can set in when faced with intrusive thoughts. These interactions will lift your spirits and give you a strong sense of support.

Creative Outlets

- **Art therapy:** Expressing your emotions and experiences through art is an incredibly therapeutic process. You can paint, draw, write, or pursue any other creative outlet you can think of. Any of these will allow you to safely explore what goes on in your head.
- **Music and movement:** Dancing, singing, or playing an instrument can be extremely powerful tools to release emotions. Something about the rhythmic movements and expressive nature of these things will have a soothing effect on your anxieties.

MANAGE TRIGGERS

These are five practical techniques that you can use to try and prevent your triggers from getting the better of you.

- **Identify your triggers:** Being aware of what sets you off is the best way to disarm your intrusive thoughts. When you get a compulsive urge, look at your environment, situation, and emotions. These triggers can be anything from certain places to certain conversations. You might even be triggered by things you feel inside. Journaling or mindfulness exercises can help you identify these triggers.
- **Challenge the thought:** OCD thrives on your fear. Whenever you have an intrusive thought, you want to keep it from taking over all your thoughts and feelings. Ask yourself if the thought has merit or if it's only being fueled by anxiety. Challenging the thoughts will often expose how irrational these intrusions are.
- **Go with the flow:** Trying to fight compulsions can feel like you're battling a current in the ocean. Instead of

fighting it, just try to ride the wave of anxiety. Let yourself feel the discomfort but try and keep yourself from acting on those thoughts. Try any of your mindfulness exercises to bring your stress levels back down.

- **Delay and disengage:** Compulsions will always feel like they are urgent, but they really aren't. Set a timer and tell yourself that you can engage in your compulsion after the timer goes off. The delay, though, is going to create just enough of a window that will disrupt the process.

- **Build your resilience:** Keep in mind that this is a long-term thing, not just a one-time fix. Taking care of yourself by getting enough sleep, eating healthy foods, and getting enough exercise every day can improve many factors of your life—including your mental health. In addition, using relaxation techniques with mindfulness practices can increase your resilience and give you the strength needed to approach new triggers.

Remember, managing these triggers is not about trying to get rid of them. You are learning how to respond to them differently than you have before. You are aware and accepting of your triggers, and you are choosing effective coping mechanisms. Again, the road is not easy, but each time you successfully handle your triggers, you become stronger and more confident. As always, if you feel like you're just spinning your wheels and not gaining any traction, do not hesitate to find help from a professional.

DEALING WITH COMPULSIONS AND INTRUSIVE THOUGHTS

It can feel like an endless fight when you're still living with these intrusive thoughts and compulsions, and it often feels like you're locked in a game of tug-of-war in your mind, especially after you've been receiving treatment. While you know that these compulsions and thoughts are driven by anxiety and fear, it doesn't make it any better when they find a way to disrupt your daily life. It's draining, but we can look back on things we have learned already and bring them together for a powerful team of tools.

The first, and most important, thing is to acknowledge that the thoughts are there. There are times when you will try to resist them, but that is mostly impossible. Pushing these thoughts away or suppressing the need to give in to your compulsion only make the feelings much more intense. This is why we are trying to promote a standpoint of responding instead of reacting. To get to a point where we respond instead of react requires changing the relationship with these thoughts.

Again, these methods have been visited before, but we are bringing them back together to help you push past the beast that is OCD.

Mindfulness and Acceptance

- **Mindfulness:** One of your best tools is going to be mindfulness because it allows you to recognize that this thought is there. Instead of playing into it as it comes, though, you will take the time to observe it.
- **Label what's happening:** When you have one of these anxieties, label it as a "compulsion" or "intrusive thought." It's a very simple way to create acceptance and a space between you and the thought. This is how you begin the process of reframing it to a response instead of a reaction.

Cognitive Reframing

- **Challenge the thoughts:** As you've learned earlier, when you become aware of your intrusive thoughts, this is the time to question their validity. Is there any evidence to back up these thoughts? Look for any evidence that you can to show that they are rooted in anxiety instead of reality.
- **Change the script:** Start to look at your compulsions as something unnecessary instead of an essential action. Along with challenging the thoughts, you will be reducing the power of the compulsion, making it easier to resist.

Self-Guided ERP

- **Face your fears:** One of your strongest tools is ERP. Slowly exposing yourself to your triggers will help you later to resist the urge to give in to your compulsions. This is a great tool, but it should go without saying that it will be scary at first. But with the right support behind you, you will be able to cut the anxiety.
- **Take it step by step:** Start very small. You don't want to jump to your biggest fear. As you conquer each little fear, you'll step up to the more difficult ones. It's all about progress, not perfection.

Get Support

- **Utilize therapy or counseling:** Finding a therapist or a counselor is beneficial as they have been trained in these fields, so they have invaluable knowledge on how to combat your OCD. You may have to spend some time sifting through resources to point you to the right person, but if you can, this is such an important piece of your journey.

- **Find others like you:** Connecting with others who understand the struggle is also extremely helpful. They can give you tips based on their own battles with OCD, or they can simply be an ear for you. Consider a support group in your area or find an online community that provides a positive environment.

CREATING A SUPPORTIVE DAILY ROUTINE

With OCD, life is dominated by anxieties and compulsions, which makes the word "routine" look terrifying. You know that having a schedule can be a great thing for daily life, and it can even help ease some of the intrusive thoughts. However, that routine can become rigid, and when you have to do this routine, you are actually giving into the cycle of compulsions and obsessions.

So how do you capture the power of routine without falling into the pitfalls of compulsion? Let's look at how routine can be beneficial to OCD and how you can create a routine that will help you along.

How Routine Can Help OCD

Most would think that routine can only make OCD worse, but when done right, it can help tremendously. When you have OCD, it's typically the uncertainty of life that triggers your anxiety. A routine can establish a sense of control and predictability, which can let you anticipate and manage situations that would have typically triggered your OCD.

Having a routine can also open up some much-needed room for healthy habits. You can make room for exercise, meditation, and other forms of self-care, which are methods that can contribute to your OCD management. They act as a barrier between your day and intrusive thoughts, and they are also great for your overall well-being.

Your routine will also promote a sense of accomplishment because, when you can stick to this routine, you will get a self-esteem boost. This is especially true for those who struggle with perfectionism and negativity. And the last real benefit to your routine is that it cuts out decision fatigue. With OCD, you are making choices in every minuscule part of your day. However, when you already have a set time for things like meals, chores, self-care, and so on, you are eliminating the opportunity for intrusive thoughts to take over.

CREATING OCD-FRIENDLY ROUTINES

Everyone's routine is going to look different, so instead, this is more of a how-to in creating a routine that works with your OCD and not against it.

- **Flexibility is crucial:** When you make a tight, rigid routine, it can lead to a new set of compulsions, which doesn't benefit your progress at all. Build in some flexibility that will allow you to make spontaneous adjustments and handle any events that come up at the last minute. You want to give yourself room to adapt without feeling guilt or anxiety.
- **Challenge instead of conforming:** Don't build a routine that plays into your compulsions. If you make a routine and some pieces feel like they are there because of your obsessions or compulsions, then you should make adjustments and introduce gradual changes.

- **Progress, not perfection:** Strive for progress instead of falling into the thinking that anything less than better is a failure. When the slip-ups do happen, be kind to yourself and remind yourself that this is all part of the process.
- **Make self-care a priority:** Make sure you're scheduling time for self-care and relaxation activities. Meditation, yoga, taking a quiet walk, and other calming activities can easily find their way into your routine. All of these can also aid in combating anxiety and improving your emotional wellness.
- **Get professional support:** Again, while treatments on their own can work, you will create more success if you have a professional backing you up. In this aspect, they can help you develop a flexible routine that puts you on the path to breaking through your OCD symptoms.

Routines can be a helpful tool, but when you try to dictate every step you take, you are confining yourself to a cage. This is meant to be an empowering tool, and it can be beneficial as you navigate the extremely complex disorder known as OCD.

And with that, we have made it through another part of your journey. These tools to help yourself can all be adjusted to benefit your symptoms, so make as many tweaks to them as you need. Now, it's time to venture into the next phase—the techniques and tips that will help you grow in your personal life!

REBUILDING RELATIONSHIPS

"Because the fight you've been waging on anxiety, all the ways you've been trying to solve, escape, or avoid it, is keeping you from the very thing you want most: to love and to be loved."

— SHEVA RAJAEE

Working on yourself and navigating the symptoms of OCD should take priority in your life. However, as you start to emerge from that grip, you have to look back on something else that was severely affected by everything you were going through—your personal relationships.

Relationships are commonly affected when it comes to OCD, which is why the first aspect, after working on yourself, is to start looking outward. By the end of this chapter, you will gain a better understanding of what OCD can do to your relationships, and you will learn some helpful skills that will help you mend fences and preserve the closeness you have with other people.

HOW OCD IMPACTS RELATIONSHIPS

By now, you have a firm grasp on the knowledge that OCD is so much more than what it's been portrayed as. This is a mental illness that casts a far-reaching shadow. While we are the most affected by this, we can't ignore that the shadow reaches our most cherished relationships. Of course, every experience is unique. Your journey is far different from mine, and those are different from someone else's, which means the impact on relationships can show itself in a lot of different ways. This creates new complexities and challenges that need to be conquered by you and those you love.

The Doubtful Shadow

Intrusive thoughts filter in, filling you with doubt about how much your partner loves you. Maybe it has you believing that you are not a worthy friend or member of your family, or perhaps you are constantly vigilant for imagined threats regarding your loved ones.

This is a manifestation that packs a huge punch when it comes to your relationships because anxiety and intrusive thoughts are embedded in the foundation of your relationships. These intrusions can lead you to need more reassurance and constant questioning, and it can even turn into controlling behaviors. This causes loved ones to pull away.

The Maze of Compulsions

When the anxiety rises, compulsions can run rampant. You've been engaging in these compulsions because you are trying to eliminate what your mind perceives as a threat. For some, the compulsions are relatively harmless, or they start out that way. But over time, and in severe cases of OCD, those compulsions become time-consuming and disruptive.

As the use of compulsions increases, it has a huge impact on your relationships. You have less time for shared activities, intimacy with your partner, and general spontaneity. For example, you plan a romantic dinner, but no one can enjoy it because of your hand washing compulsion. This can lead the other person to feel frustrated, helpless, or neglected.

Lack of Communication

Every healthy relationship thrives on open lines of communication, but OCD can come in and throw huge obstacles in those channels. When you're living in shame and the fear that goes hand-in-hand with obsessions, even opening up can be a daunting task.

Your thoughts will have you believe that you would be judged or misunderstood if you were to allow yourself to be vulnerable. In many cases, it can make you feel like you are a burden on the other person, which causes an emotional distance between you and them.

Your partner wants to be there for you, but the weight of your OCD can start to bog them down. They will experience a variety of things. The other person might be emotionally drained after constantly reassuring you or accommodating your need for compulsions. Not to mention that it's just draining for them as the outsider, so they feel depleted and unable to meet their own needs because they've been busy trying to meet the demands posed by your OCD.

IMPROVING COMMUNICATION

It should go without saying that relationships are some of the most important pillars of our lives. They offer us support and joy, and they make us feel like we really belong. With OCD, it can tear those relationships down. It does this in many ways, but the biggest impact is that of communication. Communication can solidify any bond, so without it, those relationships start to crumble.

For this section, I will walk you through some steps that can improve your general communication with your loved ones, and I will also share some insights on how you can navigate inevitable conflicts much more easily.

Communication Skills

The following are ways you can master the art of communication, even with the intrusiveness of OCD.

- **Active listening:** When you're an active listener, you aren't just hearing the words or waiting for your turn to speak. This is about paying close attention to the other person and watching their nonverbal cues. You want to truly understand their perspective because it shows them that you care and want to build a bridge of trust.
- **Use "I" statements:** Often, with OCD, it's easy to use "you" statements, which come across as accusatory. Instead of saying, "You always..." try saying, "I feel this way when this happens." This will open up a more collaborative dialogue with the other person.
- **Empathy and validation:** Allow yourself to see things from their point of view. Try to understand their feelings

and experiences with the relationship, even if you disagree. When you give them validation, you're being respectful because they feel like a real part of the conversation.

- **Use healthy nonverbal communication:** The body language you choose will speak volumes. In conversation, maintain an open posture, don't cross your arms, and try to mirror their gestures to show engagement. You should also make sure your tone is calm, even when emotions are running high. This is important because nonverbal communication can enhance or contradict what you say.
- **Use positive reinforcement:** Everyone has a desire to feel appreciated, so you should do things that show gratitude toward the other person. This will open the door for you and them to celebrate the small wins and get over the challenges posed by OCD.

Conflict Resolution

No matter how strong a relationship is, it will still have its brushes with disagreements. We can't avoid conflict, but we can choose how we handle it. That is the key that determines how resilient the bond is. So for those times when it can't be avoided, here are some resolution skills that can help calm the waters quickly.

- **Take a moment to calm down:** When things get emotional, judgment gets cloudy and things are said that shouldn't be. Take time to cool down and gather your thoughts before reengaging in the discussion. Keep in mind that charged words and aggression typically lead to escalation, not resolution.
- **Keep your focus on the issue instead of the person:** Avoid attacking or blaming the other person for the situation. You should be focused on the issue at hand and

how it has impacted you both. Word choice is important here as you need to phrase your concerns constructively and avoid generalized statements.

- **Seek common ground:** Try to find the areas where you both agree before tackling the problem. Even if it's small, when you build on your shared values, you are building an effective bridge that can generate a much more positive atmosphere. That positivity is paramount for finding solutions.
- **Practice collaborative problem-solving:** These situations involve both you and them, so you should be working together to figure out a solution that meets the needs of both parties. You should be open to compromise because the goal should be resolution and not "winning" an argument.
- **Forgive and move on:** Once you have found a resolution, that should be the end of the argument. Holding on to those feelings and grudges is only going to weigh you down. This is the time to forgive each other for anything that happened and release yourself from the burdening feelings of an argument.

FOSTERING EMPATHY

Imagine this scenario. You've had an extremely long day. You're tired and frustrated, and all you want is to have someone you can vent to and who will comfort you. However, you get home, and the person you were hoping would be there seems distant, too busy with their own thoughts. You try and open up, but their responses are all dismissive. That hurts! It makes you feel alone and like your voice doesn't matter. This is something that happens a lot in relationships because there is a lack of empathy.

Empathy is the ability to understand and share feelings. This is what connects us to another person on a much deeper level. Empathy is so much more than an intellectual understanding, though. This is stepping into the other person's shoes. You feel their happiness and sadness like it was your own. No matter the relationship type, empathy will create a much-needed layer of trust and support.

The Value of Empathy

Why is empathy so valuable to relationships, anyway?

- **Deeper understanding:** When you can empathize with someone, you are making a connection that exists beyond the surface. By being an active listener, listening to and speaking with effective nonverbal communication, and seeing things from the other person's perspective, you are creating a space with clearer communication and fewer misunderstandings.
- **Stronger emotional bonds:** Empathy fosters emotional closeness and connection. This shows the other person that you care about their feelings and that you are there to support them no matter what. By showing some emotional vulnerability, you are building more trust and reinforcing the foundation of the relationship.
- **Better conflict resolutions:** Yes, disagreements and conflict are inevitable. However, when you use an empathetic approach, you are using this as a chance to grow instead of fight. As you saw in the last section, when you work together and with empathy, you can work your way to more peaceful solutions that benefit everyone.
- **Better support:** There are so many curveballs thrown at you in life, but when someone truly understands and

empathizes with your burden, you can better navigate the darkest times.

How to Foster Empathy in Relationships

So how do you cultivate empathy in your relationships? You've already learned a lot of these steps but let's give this a good look.

- **Be an active listener:** Listen without distraction, giving the other person your full attention. And as said before, actually listen to what they're saying instead of waiting for your chance to speak.
- **Ask clarifying questions:** Don't just assume that you know where the other person is coming from. Ask open-ended questions (not "yes" or "no" questions) that will give you deeper insight into their thoughts and feelings.
- **Validate their emotions:** Acknowledge their feelings, even if you don't agree with them. Simply saying that you understand why they feel the way they do will go a long way in building more empathy.
- **Give them non-judgmental support:** No one should come from the stance of "fixing the problem." You just need to listen and be there for them. Be willing to help if they ask, but don't force your help on them.
- **Mirror their emotions:** No, you don't need to cry if someone is crying, but you should give a response that reflects theirs. If someone is crying, a hug or simple touch can make them feel validated. If they are excited, find a way to share in that enthusiasm.
- **Be vulnerable:** Never be afraid to share your feelings and experiences because this creates a space where the other person will want to do the same.

ASKING FOR SUPPORT

Open communication can be a wonderful thing, but what happens when you need support? For those who struggle with OCD, this can be difficult when your intrusive thoughts have you feeling more like a burden. Here is how you can ask for much-needed support.

1. **Timing is key:** If the other person is tired, stressed, or preoccupied, they are not going to be completely available. Try waiting for a time when things are quiet and calm and they can give you their full attention.
2. **Be clear:** Clarity is so important. Instead of hinting at what you're feeling, be direct. If you want them to listen, tell them you need an ear. Maybe you simply need a hug and some reassurance. Whatever it is, just say it.
3. **Remember your "I" statements:** Say something like, "I really need your help with…" or something similar. This will let them know that the support you're asking for is truly needed. This is how you open up a collaborative approach instead of a one-sided, unclear request.
4. **Express your appreciation:** Tell them that you appreciate their support and that they are making genuine time to give you that support. This builds more trust between both parties, which means you'll be there to support each other in the future.
5. **Accept different forms of support:** You might not get the support that you had in mind, but it doesn't mean that the other person doesn't care. That just might be how they show their support, so remember that it's the willingness to be there that matters, not the support itself.
6. **Be mindful of their boundaries:** Just because you want support doesn't mean they will be able to give it to you, or

they might not have the emotional capacity to offer that support. This doesn't mean that they are unavailable forever; it's just temporary. This is where your networking skills will pay off as you can lean on your therapist or support group. You also have boundaries, so make sure you're communicating yours as well.

It's important to know that asking for support is not a sign of weakness. If you need something and you are asking for it, you are being quite strong, actually. When you ask for support in a healthy way, you are enhancing communication, deepening connections, and navigating these challenges with the people you trust most. Never hesitate to reach out for support.

With all of these tools in mind, your relationships are going to thrive, even as you're still navigating your journey with OCD. Next up, we tackle a vital aspect of OCD, the social aspect—education and advocacy.

EDUCATION AND ADVOCACY

"Never be afraid to raise your voice for honesty and truth and compassion against injustice and lying and greed. If people all over the world... would do this, it would change the earth."

— WILLIAM FAULKNER

Education and advocacy are two forces that, when fused, can make our society a much friendlier place for those with OCD. Imagine what that would feel like when the intrusive thoughts don't trigger judgment. Instead, we are understood. A world where compulsions are met with compassion and not confusion. This is what education and advocacy can build for everyone who has to battle OCD. By shedding some light on the complexity of this condition, we can empower others who have OCD to climb their mountains, just as we have. This also allows us to be their support system.

In this chapter, you'll unlock the tools needed to become an advocate for yourself and for others. Our goal now is to foster our society to see OCD as something that needs acceptance and understanding. The more we can link together, the brighter the future will be for others who are and will be affected.

THE VALUE OF ADVOCACY

The landscape of mental health has rapidly changed in the last couple of decades. One of the biggest reasons for that evolution is advocacy, which keeps everything moving forward. In this section, we will cover what advocacy is in the context of mental health and why it's so important to us and our betterment.

What Is Advocacy?

In its simplest form, advocacy is an act of public support for a cause or a group of people. You can advocate for anything you want. When it comes to mental health issues, advocacy is actively promoting the well-being, rights, and dignity of those who are living with mental illnesses.

Advocacy can also come from a range of activities. It can come in the form of raising awareness and challenging the stigmas of mental illness, or it can be pushing for real changes that ensure all people have access to mental health services.

Let's look at what advocacy looks like for OCD specifically. This might involve:

- Sharing our personal stories of what it's like to live with OCD to argue against the misconceptions and foster some empathy.
- Lobbying for more funding into research or treatment options for those with OCD.

- Demanding that insurance companies provide better coverage for treatment options.
- Pushing back against the practices that discriminate against those who have OCD. These can include finding housing and employment.

There are also different levels of advocacy. It can be at the individual level, community, or systemic.

- Personal advocacy can be as simple as speaking openly about your own struggles with OCD. You could also ask for specific accommodations at your place of employment or push for compassionate, better-informed care from healthcare providers.
- Community advocacy typically comes in the form of showing support to a local mental health organization, taking part in awareness campaigns, or setting up support groups.
- Systemic advocacy aims to influence the policies that are in place. This advocacy looks at local, state, and national issues like inadequate resources for mental health, discriminatory laws, or the stigma that surrounds mental health.

Why Advocacy Matters

Advocacy for mental health is a priceless contribution. It's through advocacy that we can push for a positive change, which can bring a wealth of benefits to individuals, communities, and beyond. Let's look at the reasons advocacy matters so much to OCD and mental health in general.

- **It fights stigma and discrimination:** While there have been significant strides, the stigma around mental illness remains a huge barrier for those looking for help and finding that place of betterment. Advocacy's role in this is to challenge harmful stereotypes and to promote understanding and acceptance. Something as simple as sharing your personal story and highlighting your experiences with OCD can chip away at that stigma.
- **It ensures access to better care:** Access to quality mental healthcare is still a big challenge for many people. Our advocacy efforts are key for getting more funding for mental health services, broadening the availability of professionals, and ensuring that insurance policies include these essential treatments. By promoting the things that can make healthcare affordable and accessible for everyone, you are advocating for everyone's well-being.
- **It empowers individuals and communities:** Advocacy can give strength to someone else who is living with mental illness. This gives them the courage to take ownership of their stories and join in the push for real change. When someone takes ownership, they often take back that sense of control. Advocacy at the community level brings solidarity and support, which creates a network of purpose and action. When we can band together, we are creating an inclusive and supportive environment for all individuals.
- **It can change policies and legislation:** Advocacy, specifically at the systemic level, has the power to change policies and legislation at every level. When we engage with policymakers, lobbyists, and elected officials, we make the push for specific legislation, and we show them that we are holding them accountable. This can lead to a significant change in the allocation of resources, the

creation of new mental health programs, and the passing of laws that will protect the rights and dignity of all who are living with a mental illness. For example, if we are successful in our efforts to advocate for OCD, we might get more resources regarding treatments, or we can make sure that OCD is a protected disability under the ant discriminatory laws that are already in place.

ADVOCATING FOR YOURSELF AND OTHERS

This is a world filled with diverse needs and complex situations, like living with OCD, which is why there needs to be more advocates out there. When you can stand up for yourself or others, you are creating a world of understanding and positive change. For this section, I will dive in and show you how you can become an effective advocate for yourself and for those who are on their journey to find their voices.

How to Advocate for Yourself

- **Understand your worth and know your needs:** Being an advocate for yourself begins when you have a clear understanding of who you are. You are so much more than a person with OCD, so identify your strengths, boundaries, and what makes you valuable. After that, go out there and be clear about what you need and your priorities at work, in relationships, with healthcare, and so much more.
- **Gather as much information and resources as you can:** You want to be armed with knowledge, so go beyond this book and truly understand all the intricacies of OCD. Gather data, statistics, and opinions from experts that back up your argument. You will find many of your

resources in libraries, support groups, and online databases.

- **Use clear and assertive communication:** Practice expressing yourself confidently and respectfully. Work on using "I" statements and not blaming others. This is where you will also want to practice your active listening skills. This is key in getting your message across.
- **Make your goals and expectations realistic:** Much like your journey through OCD, advocacy is more like a marathon than a sprint. While setting large goals is great, you should break those down into something attainable. This will make the inevitable setbacks not so devastating. Don't forget to celebrate the wins that you get along the way.
- **Build a network:** Connect with other people who share the same concerns or who have specific expertise. This can come from support groups, professionals, or advocacy organizations, but they will all have resources, encouragement, and a community available to you.
- **Use as many methods as you can:** Think of different avenues when you want to reach an audience or raise awareness. You can write letters, set up an in-person event, or use social media to your advantage. Being persistent is also a huge step, but you have to remember to be respectful of other people's boundaries. Know your limits, too, to avoid burning yourself out.

How to Advocate with Others

- **Be an active listener and show empathy:** If you've been living with OCD, this isn't hard to do because you understand the struggles that someone else is feeling. Understanding is key to developing connections. While you do know what it's like, you should still listen attentively, ask clarifying questions, and show someone else that you really do get what they're going through.

- **Respect their autonomy and choices:** While you are being someone's voice, you have to respect their right to make their own decisions, and you have to respect the things they choose. You want to empower them and give them the same strength you found, even if their chosen path is different than yours.
- **Educate yourself about their needs:** You both may be dealing with OCD, but their specific challenges are going to be different than yours. Take the time to understand their issues, and you can share your knowledge afterward. This will help spread positive awareness.
- **Connect them with the right resources and support:** You are an advocate, which means you can't just fix someone else's problems. Your role is to guide them to relevant resources, organizations, or people that can give them the help they need. This can be pointing them toward a therapist, therapy groups, financial assistance, or even just connecting them to others who are navigating life with OCD.
- **Advocate with them, not for them:** You are empowering them, which means that you are simply the voice that they haven't found yet. You want to be a supportive guide through their journey, but you don't want to speak for them or make choices for them.
- **Work together for systemic change:** Individual advocacy is great, and getting someone else involved in community advocacy is better. However, the more individuals that join the fray, the more power we have to make broad, systemic changes. Encourage them to join as your network identifies policies, practices, or attitudes that create

barriers for others with OCD. From there, we can all finally break those barriers down.

SPREADING OCD AWARENESS

We have covered it before, but you are very likely aware of how OCD is shrouded in misconceptions and stereotypes. It can leave a person feeling isolated and misunderstood, and it can lead to some negative reactions on our part. However, when positive awareness is spread, the chains of stereotyping and misconception are broken. If you want to be part of the change, we need awareness to come from a place of positivity. Here are some ways that you can do that.

- **Share authentic stories:** Personal narratives are extremely powerful. By the time you reach this stage in your journey, you should feel empowered to share your experiences. As long as you remember this is to show the human side to OCD, and not for likes and adoration. Use social media, a blog, local support groups, or online forums. Use the opportunities you get to give an authentic retelling of the challenges and triumphs that you have experienced. Also, keep in mind that you should be respectful of other people. What that means is to allow others to tell their story and not share someone else's story without their consent.
- **Challenge the common misconceptions:** Anytime you see the stereotypical portrayal of OCD, don't be afraid to challenge it. By being educated, you will be able to educate others to see that what they see are dramatizations and not the full spectrum of the disorder. It's also helpful when you can share resources to back up your argument, which you will find during your journey.

- **Promote empathy and understanding:** Our goal through positive awareness is to shift the focus from "OCD is weird" to "OCD is human." Promote open discussions that allow you to show that this is a legitimate and treatable condition. This will also help show others that OCD is not just a cute quirk and how that portrayal is harmful to those living with OCD.
- **Be mindful of trigger words and non-inclusive language:** When talking about OCD on a broader scale, you want to avoid perpetuating the stereotypes or using trigger words that can bring up anxious feelings and intrusive thoughts in your community with OCD.
- **Support advocacy organizations:** There are so many groups out there that are dedicated to giving support to people with OCD and raising awareness on a large scale. Instead of being out there on your own, volunteer time or skills to organizations like the National Alliance on Mental Illness or even the Anxiety and Depression Association of America (ADAA). You should also join in with fundraising events or awareness events like OCD Awareness Week (check resources to find the date range).
- **Create creative content:** You might be someone who has a real gift for content creation. Writers, artists, filmmakers, and musicians can creatively spread awareness. You could even find your niche on platforms like TikTok or other social media, where you can find interesting ways to communicate what life is like with OCD. Just make sure that your portrayals are accurate and sensitive. Try to avoid harmful stereotypes or hurtful language.
- **Take part in open conversations:** If the opportunity comes to speak, then (respectfully) start a conversation about OCD in your daily life. Talk to your friends, family, and even coworkers about the challenges that you have

faced with OCD. Again, have reliable information on hand that you can pass on to someone else. This is how awareness can spread quickly and can go from the individual level to the community level and the systemic level.

Spreading awareness is so much more than just informing others about OCD; it's about making the world a place where everyone with it can feel seen, understood, and supported. When you join in and implement these strategies, you can help us break the chains of misunderstanding. You could make a difference in eliminating harmful stereotypes. This doesn't need to be a grand act. Even the smallest acts of awareness can make such a huge difference to someone else.

Mending relationships and advocating for OCD were the next steps in your journey. You're almost at the summit now! But we need to transition to the final push to the top, and this is a part that will help you keep your head up, avoid relapse, and more to ensure that your recovery efforts stay strong for the rest of your life.

RELAPSE PREVENTION

"Life does not have to be perfect to be wonderful."

— ANNETTE FUNICELLO

For a lot of people out there, the word "relapse" is something that is associated with substance abuse issues. It's an ideology that is slowly changing, but I have to bring this up because things like *recovery* and *relapse* aren't necessarily tied to substance abuse. Conditions like OCD can also be something that a person can relapse to. In this chapter, I will dive with you into the often-unseen side of OCD—relapse. We will explore its subtle forms and the steps that you can take to prevent it from taking hold of your life.

WHAT AN OCD RELAPSE LOOKS LIKE

OCD is full of the persistent whispers of intrusive thoughts, and it calls you back to your compulsions with ease. It's like a shadow, following you wherever you go, even after you've made tremendous strides in your recovery. While it seems like your progress is linear, it's not as simple as "just getting help and being better now." The reality of OCD recovery is much more complex, filled with moments of calm waters and bumpy waves. Relapsing is always a major setback, and it can stir up a lot of feelings. However, it's not something to be ashamed of. This is always a potential part of the journey, no matter how long the symptoms have stayed hidden. That's why recognizing the signs is crucial to maintain control. So let's look at how OCD can hang in the background and make its way back into your life.

The Whispers

OCD relapse comes slowly. An obsession that you thought you had conquered, and that has been dormant, suddenly turns back on. A minor thought sparks an old, familiar anxiety. For example, there are relapses where the hand washing might start to become more frequent, or the need to check to see if the doors are locked returns. These are usually minor instances, and so you brush them off. However, that's where OCD will slowly creep back in.

Anxiety Rises

The whispers don't stop; they only get louder. This is where the typical characteristics of the OCD cycle hop in. Your obsessions are there, and so are the intrusive thoughts. Both are only getting more frequent and more intrusive in your daily life. Your anxiety starts to spike because of it until you feel overwhelmed again. Before you know it, you're giving into your compulsions because you need that relief. This is where the sneakiness of OCD is so dangerous because what starts as just a thought can quickly become an act of compulsion.

OCD's Many Forms

Relapse with OCD can be tricky because it can manifest differently than your original OCD experience. This can be new themes with obsessions or evolved compulsions. You might even experience a new compulsion during relapse. For example, you were originally obsessed with cleanliness, but suddenly you are afraid that strangers can contaminate you. Maybe your need for things to be symmetrical can turn into an obsession with numerical sequences. This is where awareness of the many faces of OCD can benefit you as it can prevent a full-blown relapse.

It's not going to feel great when you realize that you have fallen back into your previous (or new) habits, but you have to remember that relapse is not a sign of weakness or failure. This is a very normal part of the recovery process, and beating yourself up for it could potentially make the situation worse. If that happens, it can be a lot harder to find help and get better coping strategies. Instead of shaming yourself, use self-compassion. Recognize that you have relapsed, but then remind yourself of how far you've come.

Think of the relapse as a new opportunity to adjust your coping strategies. Reach out to your therapist and take another look at the skills you learned during your treatment. This might be the time to re-implement ERP techniques. Sometimes it just takes revisiting what you already know to pull yourself out of a relapse.

Don't be afraid to reach out for support, either. OCD can isolate you enough, and relapse can cause a person to shut themselves down completely. You aren't alone in this, so lean on your support system—your friends, family, support groups, or therapists.

A relapse can feel like a lot, but it isn't a permanent setback. It is just an obstacle that got in your way. When you can spot the signs, remain kind to yourself, and by using your support and your tools, you can navigate this challenge and become stronger.

DEVELOPING A RELAPSE PREVENTION PLAN

Going through life with OCD can feel like making your way through a minefield of intrusive thoughts and time-consuming compulsions. One of the toughest parts of it, though, is making it through recovery only to relapse. This is why you have to remind yourself that progress with your recovery isn't going to be linear, which means relapse is a very common occurrence. However, it doesn't have to nullify all the work that you've put in already. This is where a relapse prevention plan comes in. It acts as your blueprint for navigating challenges and staying the course.

What Is a Relapse Prevention Plan?

Think of your prevention plan as a shield against your OCD. It's a personalized set of strategies and tools that will help you identify and manage stress and triggers, and it will help you resist the powerful urge to jump into your compulsions. Instead of being reactive when it happens, you are being proactive by recognizing the early warning signs and choosing an effective response method before the condition can sink its claws in.

Building Your Plan

The rest of this section will be an in-depth look at making your prevention plan. If you are seeing a therapist, consult with them before putting a plan like this into place. Also, don't forget to tailor it to your journey. There is no one-size-fits-all approach to recovery!

1. Understand Your Triggers

- **Identify your OCD themes:** What are some thoughts that keep going through your head? You want to spot the recurring thoughts, fears, and doubts that fuel the need for compulsions.
- **Zero in on your triggers:** What are some situations, emotions, or experiences that cause your OCD symptoms to fire up? For example, it could be a social gathering, or you could not be getting enough sleep.
- **Rank your triggers:** Don't forget to make a list of your triggers and organize them based on severity. This will make things easier to manage when you implement coping strategies.

2. Build Your Toolbox

- **Cognitive restructuring:** Remember that you need to challenge and reframe your intrusive thoughts with ones that are based more on reality. For example, tell yourself that instead of checking the locks multiple times, once is enough and it's okay.
- **ERP training:** One of your greatest tools is going to be exposing yourself to the triggers at a gradual pace without giving in to your compulsions. This helps you see that anxieties come and go and that you don't need your rituals.
- **Mindfulness and relaxation techniques:** Deep breathing, meditation, yoga, tai chi, and other techniques can be physical ways to manage your stress and anxiety—things that will impact your OCD symptoms.

- **Healthy habits:** Prioritizing sleep, exercise, and eating right can give you more physical boosts that can improve your mental well-being, which can make you more resilient to your OCD.
- **Build your support system:** Your network of support needs to grow. Lean on your therapist, friends, and family members. These people can encourage you, and they can guide you during the challenging points of your recovery.

3. Early Warning System

- **Know the warning signs:** More than knowing your triggers, you want to be aware of the physical, emotional, and behavioral changes you go through that send up the red flag that an OCD episode is incoming. For example, you might notice that your checking behaviors have started again.
- **Develop coping mechanisms:** Make yourself a physical list of go-to strategies that you can use when your warning signs go up. Put this in a place that is easily accessible, and when you notice these anxieties spiking, you can use them. Examples of these mechanisms are all listed above.

4. Brace for Relapse

- **Accept that setbacks are just as much a part of the journey as recovery:** Again, knowing that this can happen softens the blow when it does. Relapses are just learning opportunities, and they are great reminders that you should take time to refine your coping strategies.
- **Set up an emergency plan:** Implement a plan for the times when the symptoms can become overwhelming. Make sure to be very specific to avoid any more anxiety. This

plan could involve calling your therapist, getting to a place where you feel safe, or taking part in self-care.

5. Review and Adapt

- **Regularly review your plan:** You want to ensure that your plan always fits your needs. Remember, OCD can take on new forms, so adaptation is necessary. As you progress, adjust your plan based on your evolving needs and experiences.
- **Celebrate your successes:** Recognize yourself and all your progress and milestones, no matter how minor they are. All progress is good progress.

Building Your Worksheet

Your therapist, counselor, or even a reliable online source will have templates and worksheets that can help you create a personalized plan. This plan should be adapted to your needs, experiences, and preferences, which makes it a resonating document. Also, keep in mind that a prevention plan is a living document, so always remember that you have to review and adapt at regular intervals.

Creating your relapse prevention plan is an act of empowerment. It lets you take ownership of your well-being and keeps your tools close at hand to navigate any challenges that are brought on by your OCD.

INSPIRING SUCCESS STORIES

It's one thing to have encouragement, tools, and resources, and those are all great things. However, it can still feel daunting when you feel like it's just you against OCD. One of the best things that someone can get is inspiration from other people. The following are two stories of triumph over OCD. Names and some details have been changed, but these are tales that I've heard from other people with OCD.

The Hesitant Artist

Amelia is one of the most talented artists that you could ever meet. She could look at something and find art. You could give her a short list of items, and she'd come back with a drawing or painting that would make your jaw drop. That talent led her to be selected for a showcase at her local art show, and that's what led to her being caught in the jaws of OCD.

Every attempt at painting would be interrupted by her intrusive thoughts. Her anxieties demanded revisions and do-overs, which led to her canvases all remaining blank. The pressure to create showcase-worthy pieces turned something that brought her so much joy into an absolute burden. It was bad, but Amelia knew this was her true passion, and she refused to just give up on this opportunity.

Amelia contacted a therapist and took that brave step into recovery. She slowly learned all the tools that we've been over and learned to separate her intrusive thoughts from her talents. She started to use mindfulness techniques when her thoughts started to get too loud, and she remembered that imperfections were needed in art.

With her newfound control, Amelia went back to work. The colors flowed, and she created pieces that told stories about her battle with OCD and how she overcame it. Her showcase was a hit, and she even moved on to showcase her work in a larger gallery.

The Climber Plagued by Doubt

Evan is an adventurer. He loved hiking, skiing, biking, and anything else that got him outside. However, OCD was waiting for him when he decided to try mountain climbing. Even the smallest climbs were impossible because of the number of anxieties and doubts that he had. He had fears of contamination on top of fears about misplacing his equipment. Climbs would be slowed or canceled because of the checking and cleaning rituals that Evan would perform.

Not wanting to be grounded forever, Evan chose to take his life back. He started on a different journey, one of self-discovery. He dived into CBT with a counselor whom he found through a community center. It was here that he learned to challenge the intrusive thoughts he had, and he developed coping mechanisms that he could call in at any point. Evan went beyond CBT, too.

Evan gathered a support system of other climbers who understood his struggles. They would cheer him on, and they knew some of his early warning signs, so they were able to encourage him and empathize if he had moments where intrusive thoughts would come in. It took some time, but he slowly made his way back to the mountains.

He learned to trust his instincts and rationality, and he learned to focus on the present moment. He called on his breathing exercises whenever his anxiety began to spike. The mountains got bigger, and after a few smaller peaks, Ethan started to take on towering mountain faces.

Come back to these stories whenever you need. They are there to remind you that OCD is a powerful force, but you can overcome it. It does take courage, determination, and the right kind of support, but you can navigate the most intricate web of intrusive thoughts and reach a point of triumph.

FORWARD MOTION

"You cannot find peace by avoiding life."

— VIRGINIA WOOLF

We have gained significant ground, and the end of this book is quickly approaching, but the marathon that is life with OCD still has a long way to go. There might be something in your head right now that's wondering if this dark visitor will return, and if it does, will you be able to keep it from taking back control of your life? Fear not, because you will carry the tools of self-empowerment with you. This will act as your shield against these doubts.

Remember our hesitant artist, Amelia? She once felt overpowered by her OCD, and it left her with blank canvases. However, she is very busy with commission work and displaying her pieces in galleries today. Every piece of art she puts out is proof that goals can be more than words on a piece of paper. They can become genuine when the CLEAR tools you have are implemented.

In this chapter, we will discuss how you can keep your eyes aimed at the summit instead of looking down. You will learn how to keep your mind focused on the future instead of on the anxieties that OCD can bring.

SETTING AND ACHIEVING PERSONAL GOALS

OCD tries to dictate every move you make in life, and so far, it has been successful. But now that you're pushing on from it, you are carving a new path. This path can be filled with meaningful goals that will make a powerful statement as you reclaim control and find happiness in your life.

Setting goals is so much more than reaching a milestone; it's about asserting the dominance of your life, discovering new passions, and building a future where you are not just surviving with OCD; instead, you're thriving.

The Value of Goals

To understand the value of goals, think of your OCD as a dense fog that you can barely see through. You know there's a way out, but you don't know how to get there. Goals are like little beacons in that fog that show you there is hope, even through the fog of your anxieties. These are some of the things that your goals will give you.

- **Direction:** Without some type of destination in mind, it can be easy to just stay in the intricate web of your anxiety. Goals set that direction and give you something to stay focused on instead of what you would normally be focused on with OCD.

- **Motivation:** Even the act of setting the goal will spark something in you to push forward. That motivation can make the potential daily struggles seem like stepping stones. It leads you to the destination and adds meaning and purpose to what you're doing.
- **Confidence:** No matter how big or small, achieving a goal deserves a celebration. You reached a goal, which means you were resilient enough to keep your focus on that goal and push through. That's hard to do with OCD, so enjoy your wins!
- **Joy:** Again, you have a reason to celebrate! Reaching a goal should bring a feeling of joy into your life because you're reminded of your capabilities and the taste of success. Cherish all these moments as they will be there to remind you of your inner strengths. This will be helpful whenever you come up against an intrusive thought.

Goal-Setting Methods

Now that you know the value of goal setting, how can we turn that into action? That's a tremendous question when you are navigating the intricacies of OCD, so that's why we need some practical methods to get you started.

- **Use SMART goals:** This is a popular goal-setting method, and it ensures that your goals are Specific, Measurable, Achievable, Relevant, and Time-Bound (SMART). The best example of this would be instead of making a goal of "get in shape," you make the goal sound more like, "Jog for 20 minutes and lift weights for 30 minutes three times a week for three months." This gives you a way to track your progress, and it makes the small celebrations easier, even when you are going against OCD.

- **Values-based goals:** With this method, you align your goals with your core values. If you are a creative type, maybe your goal looks something like "draw for 15 minutes a day." When using values-based goals, you are staying motivated while remembering your sense of purpose. It's a great way to add a layer of protection against certain anxieties that may arise.
- **Visualization:** With this, you will spend a few moments each day visualizing yourself reaching your goal. Try to be as detailed as you can with this, too. See yourself reaching the goal, your celebration, and everything else that you associate with success. This is a mental rehearsal that will strengthen your resolve, give you motivation, and increase your chances of reaching success.
- **Break goals down:** We all tend to make large goals, and they can feel overwhelming at times. They can feel like a steep climb when you're living with OCD. Break your larger goal down into smaller steps that are more attainable. When you reach one of these mini-goals, your confidence will be fueled to keep you pushing forward.
- **Reward yourself:** Remember to celebrate your goals, even if they're mini ones. Your reward can be anything, like a special dinner, a long bath, time with your loved ones, or just doing something you enjoy. A reward system will reinforce positive behavior and drive your motivation.
- **Find a support system:** Sharing your goals with trusted friends, family members, or your therapist will create an environment of encouragement and accountability, which is invaluable to you.

As I've stated many times in this book, there is no one-size-fits-all approach to things, especially when it comes to goal setting. Play around with different methods and find what works best for you.

This is your journey, so your goals and the methods you choose should reflect that. Also, keep in mind that you will need to be flexible. OCD can change its forms, which could interfere with your current set of goals.

Setting and achieving goals, even with OCD hanging around, is a great act of self-affirmation. This is you telling yourself that you're not defined by your anxieties. You are defined by your dreams, resilience, and values. The path might be a challenging one, but what lies at the end is worth every moment.

REFLECTING ON THE JOURNEY

No matter where you are in the journey, it's always important to stop and do some self-reflection. Turning your focus inward and examining your experiences and patterns keeps you pointed toward understanding, acceptance, and healing.

Why Reflection Matters

Think of self-reflection as a bridge between acknowledging your struggles and taking control of your journey toward healing. It gives you the chance to step outside the whirlwind of what OCD can bring and actually look at what has been happening from a non-judgmental point of view. It's another way to look at the triggers that have fueled your obsessions and the patterns behind your compulsions. You can even peel back the layers of emotions that come with OCD. Self-reflection is a great way to untangle the web and gain insight into the ways that OCD has impacted your life.

When you achieve an understanding of your OCD, you are actually paving the way toward acceptance. Reflections help you see that OCD isn't your fault, but rather, a very real condition that you can learn to manage. Self-reflection also allows you to detach from the stigma and shame associated with OCD and mental illnesses in general, which then allows you to cultivate compassion for yourself. Accepting the experience doesn't mean that you're quietly surrendering to OCD; it shows that you acknowledge it without letting it be something that defines you. This shift in your perspective will empower you to make more rational choices when it comes to your response, and it will allow you to choose a healing method that resonates with you.

It also matters because it ignites the ever-important transformation. When you dive into the emotional sea of OCD, you can start to see the deeper fears, anxieties, and insecurities that have been feeding your compulsions for so long. By revealing and then addressing these issues, you can set yourself up for a lasting change. Think of reflection as a tranquil place to look into your vulnerabilities, challenge your limiting beliefs, and bring up new ways of thinking and coping. Use it as a way to empower yourself to rewrite the narrative of your life.

Self-Reflection Questions

If you need help finding the right questions to ask yourself when self-reflecting, you can use these prompts as a guide to help you.

- **To identify triggers:** What situations or thoughts bring up your obsessions and compulsions? Are there any common themes, situations, or emotions that are tied to these triggers?
- **When examining your compulsions:** What purpose do your compulsions serve? Are you using them as a way to get relief from the cycle of anxiety? How can you challenge these rituals and their lack of functionality?

- **Determining your values:** What are the things that truly matter to you in life? Do your OCD-related thoughts and behaviors align themselves with those core values? How can you refocus that energy? What are the things that you could do instead that would add meaning and fulfillment?
- **When thinking about your emotions:** What emotions arise when you're caught by obsessions and compulsions? Can you name them and validate them without being judgmental? What are some healthy coping mechanisms that can be used to manage your feelings?
- **For challenging beliefs:** What limiting beliefs about yourself or OCD do you hold on to? Are they realistic or helpful? How can you replace the negative self-talk with more positive affirmations and empowering phrases?
- **For celebrating progress:** How have you grown and changed since you were officially diagnosed? What coping skills do you have now? What are the things that you like to do that can be used as a way to celebrate?
- **When seeking support:** Who is there for you and is understanding, no matter what? Who can you reach out to who will provide you with a safety net?
- **When finding humor:** Can you identify moments of humor or absurdity in your experience? Much like growing, how does this differ from the place you're in now?
- **For practicing self-care:** What are the things you like doing that nourish your mind, body, and spirit? How can you incorporate those things into your daily life?
- **When you want to reframe the narrative:** Instead of seeing things as a victim, how can you make your story one of resilience and courage? What are things you have done that have proven your growth and your strengths?

These are just examples, and they are going to vary throughout your life because self-reflection is not a one-time thing. By regularly visiting these questions and keeping track of your thoughts and experiences (through journaling or other methods), you can deepen your understanding of yourself and make any adjustments in your journey that are needed. Just be patient with yourself, embrace the good and the bad, the ups and downs, and celebrate your progress as often as you can. Each day is another step to making your life your own.

EMBRACING LIFE BEYOND OCD

When you started your journey, the hope for a life beyond this relentless storm felt unattainable. You had the distressing thoughts, the intrusive urges, and your compulsive rituals that became so tangled that you couldn't see life beyond it. However, no matter how intricate the maze was, there is a way out, and there is a life where OCD will no longer be the shot-caller. While it would be nice to get rid of it completely, embracing life beyond OCD means that you know that it will never be erased. You've just learned to dance with it, and you've learned to work yourself out of those situations while taking back the joy of life.

The first step to this life beyond is acceptance. Again, acceptance doesn't mean that you are giving in to OCD; it simply means that you acknowledge that it's there and that it's a part of you. Think about throwing a party and an unwelcome guest barges in. You can't ignore that they're there, but you aren't going to let them start running the show. Your intrusive thoughts are that party crasher. You can't ignore them, but you can choose to not let them take over. This is when you disarm their power by simply observing them and letting them find their way to the door.

The next part of the life beyond is through your resilience. You know OCD thrives on fear, and it loves it when you try and ignore it. This is when it screams anxieties at you and paints worst-case scenarios in your mind. That's what gave you the urge to take part in these rituals. You thought you were keeping them away, but instead, you were being trapped by them. When it comes to getting away, you have to be resilient, and you have to embrace your ability to face your fears head-on. We went over this quite a bit, so it's up to you now. Resilience means being able to endure the discomfort and the whispers without giving in to the compulsions because it will just give them an invitation back. Every time you resist a compulsion, you are chipping away at the walls that OCD put up.

When you bring in acceptance and resilience, you have the power to rediscover your values. OCD is powerful and can easily steal your focus, making your world seem smaller and smaller. Soon, you only see the world as an OCD cycle. That causes you to forget what really matters and the things that bring you any type of joy. Use your self-reflection to take a step back. Reconnect yourself with your passions, dreams, and anything that defines your purpose. What is your spark? How can you lose yourself to healthy activities instead of the dreadful, obsessive loop? Once you find them, prioritize them. Make time for them and let them continue to show you that there really is happiness when living with OCD.

Keep in mind that the journey isn't linear. Even with life beyond OCD, there are going to be setbacks and days when the shadows come back. But when you stumble, just be compassionate to yourself. A setback is just another way to learn, which makes for another way to get stronger. Treat yourself with the same kindness and respect that you'd give the closest people in your life.

And as you move beyond OCD, remember that you're not moving on alone. There is a rich tapestry of individuals who have all walked the same path. There are so many walking alongside you now, and there will be others that follow in your footsteps. Take some time to connect with them. Share experiences, offer support, and find strength in each other's stories. This is a great place to find a reflection of the courage that you have and what life is like now as you find a new place in your journey with OCD.

You can't shake off OCD, so the life beyond it is simply embracing the journey ahead. Be better than you were the day before, and don't beat yourself down when you reach a setback. You have come so far, and there is so much more for you on the horizon.

CONCLUSION

When you picked up this book, you did so because OCD was more than just a minor inconvenience or quirk—it was an unwelcome ruler over your life. It called the shots and told you where to move and how to get there. It drained you of happiness, and it made the smallest anxieties feel like they were extremely urgent matters. When you picked this book up, you did so because you had enough. You knew that you were not meant to be trapped in this place forever.

This book has been your trusty companion on your journey, and it has equipped you with the tools and knowledge that you need to break free. It was the CLEAR framework that you needed in your map. Look back, and let's remember the steps that built that frame.

- **Comprehension:** You have gained an understanding of the nature of OCD, its triggers, and how it feeds on your intrusive thoughts *and* your compulsions.
- **Looking at you:** You learned how to face your anxieties head-on and how to dismantle the power they have over

you. You also learned to do this while practicing self-compassion and avoiding judgment.

- **Empowerment:** You have been given strength as you've reclaimed control through tools like ERP and CBT.
- **Accessing growth:** You've also gained this through the development of self-care, healthy habits, and building a support system that will be there during your recovery.
- **Recovery for life:** You also are prepared for the road ahead. You are prepared for and know how to combat setbacks and relapses. This allows you to keep OCD from taking control again.

Each chapter was a stepping stone, and each one led you closer to freedom. Together, we delved into the intrusive thoughts, compulsions, and other factors that define OCD. This helps you see them for what they are: fleeting, anxious thoughts that have no roots in reality. I helped you discover the power that acceptance can have. Acceptance can defuse the anxious thoughts that are only fueled when you engage in the compulsion. There were also tools, like ERP, that prepared you to take on the daring mission to face your anxieties without the security blanket of those compulsions.

You also learned how to nurture yourself and how to enhance your existence through physical and emotional well-being, which come together to help you withstand the power of OCD. You've also read stories based on the experiences of others, people who have fought this same monster and come out victorious, which stands as a testament to the CLEAR framework. There are also more stories out there, and you will find them through various resources; so take each of them and let them resonate with you on your journey. Soon enough, your story will be there, too.

Now, as we bring this part of your journey to a close, take a deep breath. Let everything that you have learned over the past twelve chapters settle in. This knowledge is going to be your weapon against this monster. The tools are now in your hands, and how you choose to use them is all up to you. Make the emergence from the shadow your own journey, taking it one CLEAR step at a time.

The journey so far hasn't been easy, and there are still some struggles ahead. Every one of these obstacles, though, is something that will stand as a testament to your strength. Each conquest you make will chip away at the whispers of doubt. You are more resilient than your compulsions, and you're stronger than you know. Take this knowledge and the lessons; use them to pave your future so that OCD is something that you only see as a fleeting anxiety and not the thing running your life.

And as you move forward, I have only one simple request: share your story. Let others out there know that they aren't alone in this and that there is hope waiting ahead of the cloud of doubts. Write a review, tell your story, and inspire someone else to read this book and take their first step towards a life that is their own. When we band together, OCD isn't as strong as it once was, and we will overcome it.

As this book comes to a close, remember the skills and knowledge you have learned and keep them close as you aim for the summit of your climb against OCD.

REFERENCES

Advocacy Focus. "What is Advocacy?" Advocacy Focus.(n.d.): https://advocacyfocus.org.uk/services/understanding-advocacy/

Alliance for Justice. "What is Advocacy? Definitions and Examples."(2016): https://mffh.org/wp-content/uploads/2016/04/AFJ_what-is-advocacy.pdf

Alyssa. "CommonGroup Therapy Discussion Questions." Banyan Treatment Center. (July 2, 2021): https://www.banyantreatmentcenter.com/2021/07/02/group-therapy-questions-chicago/

American Psychiatric Association. "On the Phone, In a Group, Online: New Study Evaluates Effectiveness of Different Therapy Delivery Methods."www.psychiatry.org. (August 26, 2019): https://www.psychiatry.org/news-room/apa-blogs/study-evaluates-different-therapy-delivery-models

Anwar, B. "5 Natural Remedies That Can Support OCD Treatment."TalkSpace. (June 6, 2022): https://www.talkspace.com/mental-health/conditions/obsessive-compulsive-disorder/natural-alternative-treatments/#:~:text=B%20Vitamins%3A%20Especially%20B12%20and,a%20role%20in%20neurotransmitter%20function

"Facing your fears: Exposure."Anxiety Canada.(n.d.): https://www.anxietycanada.com/sites/default/files/FacingFears_Exposure.pdf

"The Importance of Empathy in Relationships." Array Behavioral Care. (June 25, 2015): https://arraybc.com/the-importance-of-empathy-in-relationships

"How to Create a Relapse Prevention Plan." Ashley Addiction Treatment. (July 25, 2019): https://www.ashleytreatment.org/rehab-blog/relapse-prevention-plan/

MantracareAuthor. "ERP For OCD: Self Management Strategies For Obsessive-Compulsive Disorder."MantraCare.(May 3, 2022): https://mantracare.org/ocd/ocd-treatment/self-erp/

"Journaling prompts for self-reflection and recovery." Avalon Recovery Society. (August 3, 2021). https://www.avalonrecoverysociety.org/2021/08/03/journaling-prompts-for-self-reflection-and-recovery/

"Exposure Therapy and CBT for OCD Success Stories." Advanced Behavioral Health. (n.d.). Retrieved January 31, 2024: https://behaviortherapynyc.com/success-stories-ocd/#:~:text=His%20obsessive%20mind%20would%20wreak

"OCD: Myths vs reality." Benenden Health. (October 10, 2018): https://www.benenden.co.uk/be-healthy/mind/ocd-myths/

"Compulsions Don't Help: Why Doing Your Compulsions Won't You're your OCD Better."Beyond OCD. (n.d.): https://beyondocd.org/information-for-college-students/compulsion-dont-help

"Clinical definition of OCD." Beyond OCD.(2018): https://beyondocd.org/information-for-individuals/clinical-definition-of-ocd

Bilodeau, K. "Managing intrusive thoughts." Harvard Health.(October 1, 2021): https://www.health.harvard.edu/mind-and-mood/managing-intrusive-thoughts

Bonvissuto, D. "Self-Care for Living With OCD." WebMD. (2020): https://www.webmd.com/mental-health/mental-tips-living-with-ocd

Bouche, H. "The Only Question You Should Ask Your Partner When They Need Support." The Everygirl. (August 16, 2023): https://theeverygirl.com/one-question-to-ask-partner/

Bullock, G. "Present-Moment Awareness Buffers the Effects of Daily Stress." Mindful.(March 15, 2017): https://www.mindful.org/present-moment-awareness-buffers-effects-daily-stress/

Carl, E. "Guided self-help CBT, for whom is it effective?" Cognitive Behaviour Therapy.(November 1, 2019): https://www.cognbehavther.com/predictors-outcome-self-help-cbt/

Carpenter, D. "How to DevelopEmpathy in Relationships."Verywell Mind. (February 14, 2020): https://www.verywellmind.com/how-to-develop-empathy-in-relationships-1717547

Claiborn, J. "Relapse Prevention in the Treatment of OCD." International OCD Foundation. (n.d.): https://iocdf.org/expert-opinions/expert-opinion-relapse-prevention/

"Obsessive-Compulsive Disorder." Cleveland Clinic. (December 14, 2022): https://my.clevelandclinic.org/health/diseases/9490-ocd-obsessive-compulsive-disorder

Cooks-Campbell, A. "Triggered?: Learn what emotional triggers are and how to deal with them."BetterUp. (July 15, 2022): https://www.betterup.com/blog/triggers

"20 Ways to Be An Advocate for Social Change and Transformation."Courtney Harris Coaching.(October 6, 2020): https://courtneyharriscoaching.com/20-ways-to-be-an-advocate/

"The Effects of OCD on Interpersonal Relationships."Crownview Co-Occurring Institute. (May 29, 2022): https://crownviewci.com/blog/the-effects-of-ocd-on-interpersonal-relationships/

Cuncic, A. "How to Be MorePresent"Verywell Mind.(November 10, 2021): https://www.verywellmind.com/how-do-you-live-in-the-present-5204439

Curtis, M. "From Suffering in Silence, to OCD Advocacy." Made of Millions

Foundation.(n.d.): https://www.madeofmillions.com/articles/suffering-silence-ocd-advocacy

D'Arcy-Sharpe, A.-M. "A Guide to OCD Triggers." Impulse. (October 23, 2020): https://impulsetherapy.com/a-guide-to-ocd-triggers/

Daino, J. "How to Get an OCD Diagnosis."Talkspace. (n.d.): https://www.talk space.com/mental-health/conditions/obsessive-compulsive-disorder/diagno sis/#:~:text=Only%20a%20licensed%20clinician%2C%20therapist

Das, T. "Importance of self-compassion in OCD treatment."*Hindustan Times.* (September 13, 2023): https://www.hindustantimes.com/lifestyle/health/ importance-of-self-compassion-in-ocd-treatment-101694601928268.html

"Environmental Factors and OCD."BrainsWay.(May 30, 2022a): https://www. brainsway.com/knowledge-center/environmental-factors-and-ocd/

"Mindfulness and OCD."BrainsWay. (September 12, 2022b): https://www.brain sway.com/knowledge-center/mindfulness-and-ocd/

Des Marais, S. "DistortedPhysical Sensations in OCD." Psych Central.(June 16, 2022): https://psychcentral.com/ocd/distorted-physical-sensations-in-ocd

Dominguez, K. "How to Heal Through Understanding, Reflection, and Meaning."PsychoSocial. (July 5, 2020): https://psychosocial.media/2020/07/ 05/how-to-heal-through-understanding-reflection-and-meaning/

Eisner, L. "The Difference between Goals and Values and Why Both Matter." www.npaonline.com.(n.d.): https://www.npaonline.com/the-difference-between-goals-and-values-and-why-both-matter

"Additional Resources for Individuals and Families."med.emory.edu. (n.d.): https:// med.emory.edu/departments/psychiatry/programs/ocd/resources.html

Eric. "Good Habits for Mental Health."Living with OCD.(n.d.): https://www.living withocd.net/blog-1/good-habits-for-mental-health

Fagan, A. "8 Red Flags to Watch for in Therapy."www.psychologytoday.com. (October 22, 2021): https://www.psychologytoday.com/us/basics/therapy/8-red-flags-watch-in-therapy

Fallis, J. "The 22 Best Natural Treatments and Remedies for OCD." Optimal Living Dynamics. (October 17, 2023): https://www.optimallivingdynamics.com/blog/ the-22-best-natural-treatments-and-remedies-for-ocd

Farber, N. "The Value of Goals." Psychology Today.(April 19, 2012): https://www. psychologytoday.com/us/blog/the-blame-game/201204/the-value-goals

Ferguson, S. "When Relaxation Techniques Become a Compulsion." Psych Central. (July 30, 2021): https://psychcentral.com/ocd/ocd-relaxation-techniques-compulsion

Ferguson, S. "How OCD Impacts My Relationships." Psych Central. (September 28, 2022): https://psychcentral.com/ocd/ocd-impacts-relationships

Ferrando, C., and C.Selai. "A systematic review and meta-analysis on the effectiveness of exposure and response prevention therapy in the treatment of Obsessive-Compulsive Disorder."*Journal of Obsessive-Compulsive and Related Disorders*, 31, 100684. (2021): https://doi.org/10.1016/j.jocrd.2021.100684

"Whento Seek Help for OCD." FHE Health. (n.d.): https://fherehab.com/ocd/when-to-seek-help

"How to Identify and Address Intrusive Thoughts." Flourish Psychology. (September 29, 2021): https://flourishpsychologynyc.com/how-to-identify-and-address-intrusive-thoughts/

Foa, E.B. "Cognitive behavioral therapy of obsessive-compulsive disorder."*Dialogues in Clinical Neuroscience*, 12(2), 199–207.(2010): https://www.ncbi.nlm.nih.gov/pmc/articles/PMC3181959/

Frith, B. "Understanding OCD, in the workplace and beyond." Mental Health at Work. (August 19, 2022): https://www.mentalhealthatwork.org.uk/blog/under standing-ocd-in-the-workplace-and-beyond/

Geller, J. "What Is Obsessive-Compulsive Disorder?"American Psychiatric Association.(October 2022): https://www.psychiatry.org/patients-families/obsessive-compulsive-disorder/what-is-obsessive-compulsive-disorder

George, R. "Understanding and reflecting is healing."Counselling Directory. (April 27, 2022): https://www.counselling-directory.org.uk/memberarticles/under standing-and-reflecting-is-healing

Moore, M. "8 Signs aTherapist is a Bad Fit for You." Psych Central. (September 13, 2021): https://psychcentral.com/lib/red-flags-a-clinician-isnt-right-for-you

Tee-Melegrita, R.A."Ismindfulness beneficial forOCD? Research and more." Www.medicalnewstoday.com.(November 30, 2022): https://www.medicalnew stoday.com/articles/can-mindfulness-cure-ocd#:~:text=In%20a%20person%20with%20OCD

Gillihan, S.J."Discovering New Options: Self-Help Cognitive Behavioral Therapy." Nami.org.(2016): https://www.nami.org/Blogs/NAMI-Blog/November-2016/Discovering-New-Options-Self-Help-Cognitive-Behav#:~:text=It

Glazier, K., M. Swing, and L.K.McGinn. "Half of Obsessive-Compulsive Disorder Cases Misdiagnosed."*The Journal of Clinical Psychiatry*, 76(06), e761–e767. (2015): https://doi.org/10.4088/jcp.14m09110

Guarnotta, E. "Medication for OCD: Types, Side Effects, & Effectiveness." Choosing Therapy. (January 11, 2024): https://www.choosingtherapy.com/medication-for-ocd/#:~:text=SSRIs%20like%20Zoloft%2C%20Prozac%2C%20and,first%20medications%20recommended%20for%20OCD.&text=These%20medications%20are%20considered%20to,possibility%20of%20developing%20suicidal%20thoughts

Gupta, S. "How DoesExposure Therapy?"Verywell Mind. (June 29, 2021): https://

www.verywellmind.com/exposure-therapy-definition-techniques-and-effi cacy-5190514

Harrison, S. "What Does Self-Compassion Really Mean?"*Harvard Business Review.* (December 12, 2022): https://hbr.org/2022/12/what-does-self-compassion-really-mean

"82 Best Quotes About Advocacy." Good GoodGood.(September 4, 2023): https://www.goodgoodgood.co/articles/advocacy-quotes

Headspace Mindfulness and Meditation Experts. "What is mindfulness?" Headspace. (2020): https://www.headspace.com/mindfulness/mindfulness-101

HealthMatch staff. "How To Spread Awareness About OCD."HealthMatch. (September 22, 2022): https://healthmatch.io/ocd/how-to-spread-ocd-awareness

Hershfield, J. "How to Respond to Unwanted, Obsessive Thoughts." Sheppard Pratt. (July 23, 2017): https://www.sheppardpratt.org/news-views/story/how-to-respond-to-unwanted-obsessive-thoughts/

Hershfield, J., and T.Corboy. "Mindfulness and Cognitive Behavioral Therapy for OCD."International OCD Foundation. (2010): https://iocdf.org/expert-opin ions/mindfulness-and-cognitive-behavioral-therapy-for-ocd/

Higa, K. "10 Reasons Why Advocacy is Important." Human Rights Careers. (July 28, 2022): https://www.humanrightscareers.com/issues/why-advocacy-is-important/#:~:text=By%20advocating%20for%20a%20cause

Hildebrandt, J. "Finding My Feet in the Face of Relapse."Made of Millions Foundation.(n.d.). Retrieved January 31, 2024: https://www.madeofmillions. com/articles/finding-my-feet-in-the-face-of-relapse

Himani. "OCD Relapse: What Is It And How To Avoid" Mantra Care. (May 7, 2022): https://mantracare.org/ocd/ocd-treatment/ocd-relapse/

Hoffman, J.K."Finding Release Through Art Therapy." Made of Millions Foundation.(n.d.): https://www.madeofmillions.com/articles/finding-ocd-release-through-art-therapy

Hollander, E. "5 Ways to Break the OCD Stigma." Psychology Today. (April 8, 2019): https://www.psychologytoday.com/us/blog/overcoming-obsessions-and-shifting-focus/201904/5-ways-break-the-ocd-stigma

Huey, E.D., R. Zahn, F. Krueger, J. Moll, D.Kapogiannis, E.M. Wassermann, and J. Grafman. "A Psychological and Neuroanatomical Model of Obsessive-Compulsive Disorder."*Journal of Neuropsychiatry*, 20(4), 390–408.(2008): https://doi.org/10.1176/appi.neuropsych.20.4.390

Hughes, J. "10 Ways to Advocate for Those With OCD."www.justinkhughes.com. (July 7, 2023): https://www.justinkhughes.com/jog/10-ways-to-advocate-for-those-with-ocd/

Hutchinson, S. "How to Write a Bulletproof Relapse Prevention Plan." River Oaks. (April 25, 2023): https://riveroakstreatment.com/drug-treatment/relapse-prevention-plan/

"How is OCD Diagnosed?" International OCD Foundation. (2010): https://iocdf. org/about-ocd/how-is-ocd-diagnosed/

"Who Gets OCD?"International OCD Foundation.(2023): https://iocdf.org/about-ocd/who-gets-ocd/

"What Causes OCD?" International OCD Foundation. (n.d.): https://iocdf.org/about-ocd/what-causes-ocd/#:~:text=Research%20suggests%20that%20OCD%20involves

"How Do I Find Help for OCD?" International OCD Foundation. (2010a): https://iocdf.org/ocd-finding-help/

"How to Find the Right Therapist." International OCD Foundation. (2010b): https://iocdf.org/ocd-finding-help/how-to-find-the-right-therapist/

"Medications for OCD." International OCD Foundation. (2010c): https://iocdf. org/about-ocd/treatment/meds

"Guest post: Wendy Mueller Shares Her Recovery Success Story." International OCD Foundation. (October 13, 2015): https://iocdf.org/blog/2015/10/13/guest-post-wendy-mueller-shares-her-recovery-success-story/

"OCD Awareness Week is here! How can you get involved?" International OCD Foundation. (October 10, 2016): https://iocdf.org/blog/2016/10/10/ocdweek-2016/

"10 Ways to Be an OCD Advocate." International OCD Foundation. (January 19, 2022): https://iocdf.org/blog/2022/01/19/10-ways-to-be-an-ocd-advocate/

"Obsessive-Compulsive Disorder (OCD)."Johns Hopkins Medicine. (2022): https://www.hopkinsmedicine.org/health/conditions-and-diseases/obsessive compulsive-disorder-ocd

Jones, H. "A Practical Guide to Meditation for OCD?"Verywell Health. (May 19, 2022): https://www.verywellhealth.com/meditation-for-ocd-how-to-guide-5220556#:~:text=Slowly%20breathe%20in%20deeply%20from

Jones, R. "35 OCD (Obsessive-Compulsive Disorder) Quotes About Dealing With Challenges." Happier Human. (May 24, 2023): https://www.happierhuman. com/ocd-quotes-rj1/

Juma, N. "OCD quotes for Those with this Difficult Disorder." Everyday Power. (February 24, 2023): https://everydaypower.com/ocd-quotes/

Kastens, A. "5 roadblocks to Acceptance in the Treatment of OCD."PsychologyToday.(December 20, 2019): https://www.psychologytoday. com/us/blog/all-things-anxiety/201912/5-roadblocks-acceptance-in-the-treatment-ocd

Kastens, A. "The Physical Impacts of OCD." NOCD. (January 5, 2023): https://www.treatmyocd.com/blog/the-physical-impacts-of-ocd

Kelly, O. "Exposure Therapy for OCD."Verywell Mind. (November 23, 2023a): https://www.verywellmind.com/exposure-therapy-for-ocd-2510616

Kelly, O. "Herbal Remedies for OCD and Anxiety."Verywell Mind. (December 6, 2023b): https://www.verywellmind.com/herbal-remedies-for-ocd-2510631

Khan, I., Taimoor Asif Jaura, Alaa Tukruna, A. Arif, , Sameer Saleem Tebha, S. Nasir, D. Mukherjee, N. Masroor, and Abubakr Yosufi. "Use of Selective Alternative Therapies for Treatment of OCD."*Neuropsychiatric Disease and Treatment.19*, 721–732. (2023): https://doi.org/10.2147/ndt.s403997

Kissen, D. "How to Take the Power Back from Intrusive Thought OCD."Adaa.org. (2019): https://adaa.org/learn-from-us/from-the-experts/blog-posts/consumer/how-take-power-back-intrusive-thought-ocd

Kohler, K.C., B.J. Coetzee, and C. Lochner. "Living with obsessive-compulsive disorder (OCD): a South African narrative."*International Journal of Mental Health Systems*, 12(1). (2018): https://doi.org/10.1186/s13033-018-0253-8

Krebs, G.C., L.J. Hannigan, A.M. Gregory, F.V. Rijsdijk, B. Maughan, and T.C. Eley. "Are punitive parenting and stressful life events environmental risk factors for obsessive-compulsive symptoms in youth? A longitudinal twin study."*European Psychiatry*, *56*(1), 35–42. (2018): https://doi.org/10.1016/j.eurpsy.2018.11.004

Langham, D.R.Y. "How to Recover From an OCD Relapse." Impulse. (November 4, 2022): https://impulsetherapy.com/how-to-recover-from-an-ocd-relapse/

Law, C., and C.L.Boisseau. "Exposure and Response Prevention in the Treatment of Obsessive-Compulsive Disorder: Current Perspectives."*Psychology Research and Behavior Management*, 12(1167–1174), 1167–1174. (2019): https://doi.org/10.2147/prbm.s211117

Levy, J., and J.Weiner. "Pure O: An Exploration into a Lesser-known Form of OCD." Made of Millions Foundation. (n.d.): https://www.madeofmillions.com/articles/pure-o-an-exploration-into-a-lesser-known-form-of-ocd

Lock, H. "What Actually Is 'Advocacy' and How Can We All Use it to Change the World?" Global Citizen.(August 17, 2021): https://www.globalcitizen.org/en/content/what-is-advocacy/

"The ultimate goal setting process: 7 steps to creating better goals."Lucidchart. (February 6, 2018): https://www.lucidchart.com/blog/7-steps-to-creating-better-goals

Lyness, D. "Obsessive-Compulsive Disorder (OCD)."KidsHealth.(2017): https://kidshealth.org/en/teens/ocd.html

"Stigma and OCD." Made of Millions Foundation.(n.d.-a): https://www.madeofmillions.com/ocd/stigma-and-ocd

"Work and OCD." Made of Millions Foundation. (n.d.-b): https://www.madeofmil lions.com/ocd/work-and-ocd#:~:text=OCD%20issues%20in%20the% 20workplace

Makin, S. "Therapies for OCD: Discover The 10 Best Standard And Alternative Options." Makin Wellness. (March 17, 2023): https://www.makinwellness. com/therapies-for-ocd/

"Obsessive-compulsive disorder (OCD)."Mayo Clinic. (2016): https://www. mayoclinic.org/diseases-conditions/obsessive-compulsive-disorder/diagnosis-treatment/drc-20354438

"Obsessive-compulsive disorder (OCD)."Mayo Clinic. (2020): https://www. mayoclinic.org/diseases-conditions/obsessive-compulsive-disorder/symp toms-causes/syc-20354432

McGrath, P. "What Is Exposure and Response Prevention Therapy?"NOCD. (n.d.): https://www.treatmyocd.com/what-is-ocd/what-is-erp

McGrath, P. "Should I First Try ERP on My Own?"NOCD. (April 25, 2020): https://www.treatmyocd.com/blog/should-i-first-try-erp-on-my-own

McGrath, P. "What Tests Are Used to Diagnose OCD?"NOCD. (January 29, 2021): https://www.treatmyocd.com/blog/what-tests-are-used-to-diagnose-ocd

McLaughlin, S. "How To Become An Advocate (You May Already Be One!)."Pathfinders for Autism. (n.d.): https://pathfindersforautism.org/articles/ advocacy/how-to-become-an-advocate-you-may-already-be-one/#:~: text=When%20advocating%20for%20others%2C%20always

"Everything You Need to Know aboutExposure and Response Prevention Therapy."McLean Hospital. (n.d.): https://www.mcleanhospital.org/ essential/erp

Knose, A. "Meditation for OCD: Benefits, Techniques, &Exercises to Try."Choosing Therapy. (July 19, 2023): https://www.choosingtherapy.com/ meditation-for-ocd/

"Obsessive compulsive Disorder (OCD) Test."MedlinePlus.(n.d.): https://medline plus.gov/lab-tests/obsessive-compulsive-disorder-ocd-test/

Mehta, S. "15 EffectiveGoal Setting Methods: Framework and Systems."Peoplebox. (December 14, 2021): https://www.peoplebox.ai/blog/different-goal-setting-methods/

Menon, J., and A.Kandasamy. "Relapse prevention."*Indian Journal of Psychiatry*, 60(4), 473–478. (2018): https://doi.org/10.4103/psychiatry.IndianJPsychiatry_36_18

"What is OCD?"Mind.(2019a): https://www.mind.org.uk/information-support/ types-of-mental-health-problems/obsessive-compulsive-disorder-ocd/about-ocd/

"How can I help someone with OCD?"Mind.(2019b): https://www.mind.org.uk/

information-support/types-of-mental-health-problems/obsessive-compul
sive-disorder-ocd/for-friends-family/

"How can I help myself with OCD?"Mind.(May2019c). https://www.mind.org.uk/
information-support/types-of-mental-health-problems/obsessive-compul
sive-disorder-ocd/self-care-for-ocd/

"About mindfulness."Mind.(2021): https://www.mind.org.uk/information-
support/drugs-and-treatments/mindfulness/about-mindfulness/

Mindful Staff. "What is Mindfulness?" Mindful. (July 8, 2020): https://www.mind
ful.org/what-is-mindfulness/

"Discussion Questions for OCD." Mission Peak Unitarian Universalist
Congregation.(n.d.): https://mpuuc.org/obsessive-compulsive-disorder-ocd/
discussion-questions-ocd/

Munford, P.R."Self-Directed Treatment for OCD: The Irony of Doing the
Opposite." International OCD Foundation.(n.d.): https://iocdf.org/expert-opin
ions/expert-opinion-self-directed-erp/

"*Obsessive-Compulsive disorder: Should I take medicine for OCD?*"My Health Alberta.
(n.d.): https://myhealth.alberta.ca/Health/Pages/conditions.aspx?hwid=ty6699

"Diagnostic criteria for OCD in ICD-10 and DSM-IV."National Library of
Medicine(2006): https://www.ncbi.nlm.nih.gov/books/NBK56452/

"Obsessive-Compulsive Disorder."National Institute of Mental Health. (October
2019): https://www.nimh.nih.gov/health/topics/obsessive-compulsive-disor
der-ocd

"Why Advocacy Matters."National Kidney Foundation. (n.d.): https://www.kidney.
org/sites/default/files/Why-Advocacy-Matters.pdf

"Seven Conflict Resolution Tips for Couples." National University. (November 20,
2018): https://www.nu.edu/blog/seven-conflict-resolution-tips-for-couples/

"What are intrusive thoughts, and are they normal?"Nebraska Med. (June
13,2023): https://www.nebraskamed.com/behavioral-health/health/condi
tions-and-services/what-are-intrusive-thoughts-and-are-they-normal#:~:
text=Intrusive%20thoughts%20are%20ideas%20and

Neff, K. "Self-Compassion." Self-Compassion. (2019): https://self-compassion.
org/the-three-elements-of-self-compassion-2/

"Symptoms – Obsessive compulsive disorder (OCD)."NHS.(February 16, 2021):
https://www.nhs.uk/mental-health/conditions/obsessive-compulsive-disor
der-ocd/symptoms/

"Overview– obsessive compulsive disorder (OCD)." NHS. (April 4, 2023): https://
https//www.nhs.uk/mental-health/conditions/obsessive-compulsive-disor
der-ocd/symptoms/www.nhs.uk/mental-health/conditions/obsessive-compul
sive-disorder-ocd/overview/

"Aha! Moments from Self-Compassion."Shala. (May 1, 2015): https://www.shalan icely.com/aha-moments/aha-moments-from-self-compassion/

"What's The Difference Between Cognitive-Behavioral Therapy, Exposure Therapy, And Exposure With Response Prevention?" OCD & Anxiety Center of Cleveland. (September 24, 2018): https://ocdandanxietycenterofcleveland. com/anxietyblog/2018/9/24/whats-the-difference-between-cognitive-behav ioral-therapy-and-exposure-with-response-prevention-and-exposure-therapy

"Diagnostic and Statistical Manual of Mental Disorders and OCD."OCD UK. (2013): https://www.ocduk.org/ocd/clinical-classification-of-ocd/dsm-and-ocd/

"The Impact of OCD."OCD UK. (2018a): https://www.ocduk.org/ocd/impact-of-ocd/

"What is Cognitive Behavioural Therapy (CBT)?"OCD UK.(2018b): https://www. ocduk.org/overcoming-ocd/cognitive-behavioural-therapy/

"What are compulsions?" OCD UK. (n.d.): https://www.ocduk.org/ocd/ compulsions/

Ohlin, B. "7 ways to Improve Communication in Relationships."PositivePsychology. (July 4, 2019): https://positivepsychology. com/communication-in-relationships/

Olivardia, R. "How Is OCD Diagnosed? Understanding the evaluation process."Attitude. (May 27, 2021): https://www.additudemag.com/how-is-ocd-diagnosed/

Orbuch, T. "How to Ask Your Partner for the Support You Need." Paired. (n.d.). Retrieved January 31, 2024: https://www.paired.com/articles/how-to-ask-your-partner-for-the-support-you-need

"What Is OCD?" Orchard. (June 7, 2022): https://www.orchardocd.org/comple mentary-and-alternative-therapies/#:~:text=In%20general%2C%20the% 20results%20of

Pace, R. "10 Effective Communication Skills in Relationships."Marriage.com. (January 11, 2018): https://www.marriage.com/advice/relationship/effective-relationship-communication-skills/

Pace, R. "How to Build Empathy in Relationships." Marriage.com. (February 18, 2021): https://www.marriage.com/advice/relationship/how-to-build-empa thy-in-relationships/

Pedersen, T. "What is an OCD Trigger?" Psych Central. (May 17, 2016): https:// psychcentral.com/ocd/what-is-an-ocd-trigger

Pedersen, T. "What causes Obsessive-Compulsive Disorder (OCD)?" Psych Central. (June 8, 2021): https://psychcentral.com/ocd/what-causes-obsessive-compulsive-disorder-ocd#:~:text=Environmental%20factors%20such%20as% 20stress

Pedersen, T. "What Are Triggers and How Do They Form?" Psych Central. (April 28, 2022): https://psychcentral.com/lib/what-is-a-trigger

"Understanding CBT for OCD."Penn Psychiatry. (n.d.): https://www.med.upenn.edu/ctsa/forms_ocd_cbt.html#:~:text=Cognitive%2Dbehavior%20therapy%20is%20a

"Understanding CBT for OCD"Penn Psychiatry. (2022): https://www.med.upenn.edu/ctsa/forms_ocd_cbt.html

Penzel, F. "Acceptance and OCD." Beyond OCD. (n.d.): https://beyondocd.org/expert-perspectives/articles/acceptance-and-ocd#:~:text=Accepting%20Your%20Illness%20and%20its

Penzel, F. "25 Tips for Succeeding in Your OCD Treatment." International OCD Foundation. (2014): https://iocdf.org/expert-opinions/25-tips-for-ocd-treatment/

Perez, M.I., D.L. Limon, A.E. Candelari, S.L. Cepeda, A.C. Ramirez, A.G. Guzick, M. Kook, M., V. La Buissonniere Ariza, S.C. Schneider, W.K. Goodman, and E.A. Storch. "Obsessive-compulsive disorder misdiagnosis among mental healthcare providers in Latin America."Journal of Obsessive-Compulsive and Related Disorders, 32, 100693. (2022): https://doi.org/10.1016/j.jocrd.2021.100693

Ponte, K. "Understanding Mental Health Triggers." Campus Health. (January 27, 2022): https://campushealth.unc.edu/health-topic/understanding-mental-health-triggers/

"Exposure and Response Prevention."Psychology Today. (n.d.-a): https://www.psychologytoday.com/us/therapy-types/exposure-and-response-prevention

"Find an Obsessive-Compulsive (OCD) Therapist."Psychology Today. (n.d.-b): https://www.psychologytoday.com/us/therapists/obsessive-compulsive-ocd

"The Hidden Silver Linings Of OCD."Pulse TMS. (August 21, 2020): https://pulsetms.com/blog/the-hidden-silver-linings-of-ocd/#:~:text=Some%20studies%20have%20suggested%20that

Quick, S. "What does it actually mean for OCD to be 'triggered'?" NOCD. (May 17, 2022a): https://www.treatmyocd.com/blog/what-does-it-actually-mean-for-ocd-to-be-triggered

Quick, S. "Why does my OCD keep switching themes?" NOCD. (October 3, 2022b): https://www.treatmyocd.com/blog/why-does-my-ocd-keep-switching-themes

Quick, S. "The importance of self-compassion when you have OCD." NOCD. (March 29, 2023a): https://www.treatmyocd.com/blog/the-importance-of-self-compassion-when-you-have-ocd

Quick, S. "How can I tell if a thought is intrusive?"NOCD. (April 3, 2023b): https://www.treatmyocd.com/blog/how-can-i-tell-if-a-thought-is-intrusive

Quinn, D. "Exposure and response prevention: 5+ ERP techniques." Sandstone Care. (December 23, 2023): https://www.sandstonecare.com/blog/exposure-response-prevention-erp/

Rajaee, S. "Relationship OCD Quotes."Goodreads. (n.d.): https://www.goodreads.com/work/quotes/88607324-relationship-ocd-a-cbt-based-guide-to-move-beyond-obsessive-doubt-anxi

Rapp, A.M., R.L. Bergman, J. Piacentini, and J.F.Mcguire. "Evidence-Based Assessment of Obsessive–Compulsive Disorder."*Journal of Central Nervous System Disease*, 8, 13–29. (2016): https://doi.org/10.4137/jcnsd.s38359

Reid, S. "Empathy: How to Feel and Respond to the Emotions of Others."HelpGuide.(October 11, 2023): https://www.helpguide.org/articles/relationships-communication/empathy.htm#:~:text=Empathy%20helps%20you%20see%20things

Rickardsson, J. "5 Reasons why empathy is important in relationships." 29k. (n.d.-a): https://29k.org/article/5-reasons-why-empathy-is-important-in-relationships

Rickardsson, J. "Ways to develop empathy in a relationship." 29k. (n.d.-b): https://29k.org/article/ways-to-develop-empathy-in-a-relationship

Ridley, C., and H. DeWitt. "Is OCD genetic? Causes and treatments for OCD?"Thriveworks. (April 12, 2023): https://thriveworks.com/help-with/obsessive-compulsive-disorder-ocd/is-ocd-genetic/

Riopel, L. "The importance, Benefits, and Value of Goal Setting."PositivePsychology. (June 14, 2019): https://positivepsychology.com/benefits-goal-setting/#:~:text=Setting%20goals%20and%20working%20to

Rodriguez, R.J."Breaking out of routine - obsessive compulsive disorder." Dr. Raul J. Rodriguez. (March 9, 2015): https://www.delraybeachpsychiatrist.com/breaking-routine-obsessive-compulsive-disorder/

Ryu, J. "7 Therapist Red Flags You Should Never Ignore."SELF. (July 26, 2023): https://www.self.com/story/therapist-red-flags

Saripalli, V. "How Can OCD Affect Your Work life? Plus 4 Coping Tips." Psych Central. (October 14, 2013): https://psychcentral.com/ocd/ocd-and-employment

Schuster, S. "17 Quotes That Prove OCD Is So Much More Than Being Neat." The Mighty. (October 19, 2023): https://themighty.com/topic/obsessive-compulsive-disorder-ocd/what-ocd-feels-like/

Scott, E. "Conflict Resolution Skills and Strategies for Healthy Relationships."VerywellMind. (February 6, 2008): https://www.verywellmind.com/conflict-resolution-skills-for-healthy-relationships-3144953

Seay, S. "OCD Triggers in Daily Life? Don't Ritualize. Be Strategic! 3 Tips for Fighting OCD." Center for Psychology and Behavior Science. (n.d.): https://

www.psychologyandbehavior.com/ocd-triggers-erp-tips-pure-o/

Seif, M., and S.Winston. "Unwanted Intrusive Thoughts." ADAA. (2019): https://adaa.org/learn-from-us/from-the-experts/blog-posts/consumer/unwanted-intrusive-thoughts

Shapiro, L. "OCD: Everything You Need To Know About OCD."McLean. (August 27, 2023): https://www.mcleanhospital.org/essential/ocd#:~:text=These%20thoughts%20and%20compulsions%20are

Shinar, D.O. "Dr. Ori's OCD Success Stories." Dr. Ori. (December 13, 2021): https://psychologistsnyc.com/dr-oris-ocd-success-stories/

Simkus, J. "What Is Exposure And Response Prevention (ERP) Therapy?" Simply Psychology. (April 18, 2023): https://www.simplypsychology.org/what-is-exposure-and-response-prevention-therapy.html

Simpson, H.B., and D.M.Hezel. "Exposure and response prevention for obsessive-compulsive disorder: A review and new directions."*Indian Journal of Psychiatry*, 61(7), 85–92. (2019): https://doi.org/10.4103/psychiatry.indianjpsychiatry_516_18

Smith, E. "Life After, Life After OCD."International OCD Foundation. (January 15, 2019): https://iocdf.org/blog/2019/01/15/life-after-life-after-ocd/

Smith, K. "OCD Medication Guide."Psycom. (October 8, 2020): https://www.psycom.net/ocd-medication-guide

Smith, S. "Distraction: Helpful or Unhelpful When Treating OCD?" StacySmithCounseling. (March 27, 2019): https://www.stacysmithcounseling.com/post/distraction-helpful-or-unhelpful-when-treating-ocd

Smith, S. "Instead Of Yearning For Your Old Life Back, Live Better Now." NOCD. (September 8, 2021): https://www.treatmyocd.com/blog/instead-of-yearning-for-your-old-life-back-live-better-now

Society for Neuroscience. "Why Your Advocacy Matters."(n.d.). Retrieved January 31, 2024: https://www.sfn.org/-/media/SfN/Documents/NEW-SfN/Advocacy/Best-Practices/190074_Why-Your-Advocacy-Matters.pdf

Sommers, J. "My journey to Hell and Back, A Personal Experience with CBT and ERP." International OCD Foundation. (August 27, 2013): https://iocdf.org/blog/2013/08/27/my-journey-to-hell-and-back-a-personal-experience-with-cbt-and-erp/

Stahl, M. "Creativity and OCD Go Bizarrely Hand-In-Hand."*Vice*. (October 4, 2017): https://www.vice.com/en/article/43a5eq/creativity-and-ocd-go-bizarrely-hand-in-hand

Stahnke, B. "A systematic review of misdiagnosis in those with obsessive-compulsive disorder."*Journal of Affective Disorders Reports*, 6(1), 100231. (2021): https://doi.org/10.1016/j.jadr.2021.100231

"Self-Compassion."Stanford Medicine. (n.d.-a): https://ccare.stanford.edu/

research/wiki/compassion-definitions/self-compassion/

"Understanding OCD."Stanford Medicine. (n.d.-b): https://med.stanford.edu/ocd/about/understanding.html

"Goal Setting Techniques And Strategies You Can Use Now For Future Success."NSLS. (n.d.): https://www.nsls.org/goal-setting-techniques

Sutton, J. "Conflict Resolution in Relationships and Couples: 5 Strategies."PositivePsychology.(November 9, 2021): https://positivepsychology.com/conflict-resolution-relationships/

Szymanski, J. "What Are Common Obsessions and Compulsions?" EverydayHealth. (n.d.): https://www.everydayhealth.com/anxiety-disorders/experts-common-obessions-and-compulsions.aspx

Talago, L. "How to Create a Relapse Prevention Plan to Maintain Your Recovery."GoodRx. (February 8, 2023): https://www.goodrx.com/conditions/substance-use-disorder/relapse-prevention-plan

Tartakovsky, M. "How to Ask Your Spouse for Support—Without Sounding Like a Nag or Critic."Psych Central. (January 4, 2019): https://psychcentral.com/lib/how-to-ask-your-spouse-for-support-without-sounding-like-a-nag-or-critic#1

"Relationship OCD –Symptoms &Treatment."The Gateway Institute.(n.d.): https://www.gatewayocd.com/relationship-ocd-symptoms-and-treatment/#:~:text=Relationship%20OCD%2C%20or%20rOCD%2C%20is

"Contamination OCD –Symptoms and Treatment." The Gateway Institute. (October 16, 2027): https://www.gatewayocd.com/contamination-ocd-symptoms-and-treatment/

"How to Improve Communication Skills in Your Relationship." The Jed Foundation. (n.d.): https://jedfoundation.org/resource/how-to-improve-communication-skills-in-your-relationship/

"Reduce Stress by Being Present." The Monday Campaigns. May 16, 2022): https://www.mondaycampaigns.org/destress-monday/reduce-stress-by-being-present

"National Experts in treatment for OCD, Anxiety, and Trauma."OCD Anxiety Centers. (November 25, 2023): https://www.theocdandanxietytreatmentcenter.com/#:~:text=Practicing%20self%2Dcompassion%20can%20have

"7 Common Myths About OCD." The Recovery Village Drug and Alcohol Rehab. (May 26, 2022): https://www.therecoveryvillage.com/mental-health/ocd/ocd-myths/

"How to Be an Advocate for Yourself and Others." The Well Project. (March 18, 2019): https://www.thewellproject.org/hiv-information/how-be-advocate-yourself-and-others

"Relapse Prevention Plan (Version 2) (worksheet)."Therapist Aid. (n.d.): https://www.therapistaid.com/therapy-worksheet/relapse-prevention-plan-2

Truong, K. "Why Your Love Of Routines Probably Isn't OCD."Refinery29. (August 31, 2018): https://www.refinery29.com/en-us/daily-routines-obsessive-compulsive-disorder-signs

"Strategies to Redirect Your Thoughts and Distract Your Mind."University Hospitals. (April 24, 2020): https://www.uhhospitals.org/blog/articles/2020/04/strategies-to-redirect-your-thoughts-and-distract-your-mind

"Exposure and Desensitization."UMich.(n.d.): https://medicine.umich.edu/sites/default/files/content/downloads/Exposure-and-Desensitization.pdf

"Recognizing relapse."UNC School of Medicine. (n.d.): https://www.med.unc.edu/psych/cecmh/archived-old-pages/recognizing-relapse/

"The Impact of OCD on Relationships." United Brain Association.(July 24, 2019): https://unitedbrainassociation.org/2019/07/24/the-impact-of-ocd-on-relationships/

"Reflective Practices."University of Minnesota, Bakken Center for Spirituality & Healing. (n.d.): https://csh.umn.edu/academics/whole-systems-healing/reflective-practices#:~:text=Reflective%20practices%20are%20a%20way

Valentine, D.K. "What to know when finding a therapist for OCD." NOCD. (November 30, 2023): https://www.treatmyocd.com/blog/how-to-find-an-ocd-therapist

Valentine, K. "How Long Does ERP Therapy Take?" NOCD. (January 6, 2021): https://www.treatmyocd.com/blog/how-long-does-erp-therapy-take

Victoria State Government. "*Obsessive compulsive disorder.*"Better Health Channel. (2012): https://www.betterhealth.vic.gov.au/health/conditionsandtreatments/obsessive-compulsive-disorder

Wade, D. "Exposure Response Prevention Therapy for OCD: Does It Work?" Psych Central. (August 11, 2021): https://psychcentral.com/ocd/exposure-erp-therapy-for-ocd

"Quotations for OCD." Western Suffolk Psychological Services. (n.d.): https://www.wsps.info/quotations-for-ocd

Whittal, M.L., D.S. Thordarson, and P.D. McLean. "Treatment of obsessive–compulsive disorder: Cognitive behavior therapy vs. exposure and response prevention."*Behaviour Research and Therapy*, 43(12), 1559–1576. (2005): https://doi.org/10.1016/j.brat.2004.11.012

Wilcox, E. "A Morning Routine with OCD." ILLUMINATION. (January 5, 2021): https://medium.com/illumination/a-morning-routine-with-ocd-25ef5a84282b

"Moving Beyond OCD, Just Once." Yeah OCD. (November 30, 2019): https://yeahocd.com/moving-beyond-ocd-just

Zauderer, S. "57+ OCD Statistics: How Many People Have OCD?"CrossRiverTherapy.(January 11, 2023): https://www.crossrivertherapy.com/ocd-statistics#:~:text=People%20Have%20OCD%3F-

Made in the USA
Las Vegas, NV
15 September 2024

95288179R00085